Are You a Target?

The Wadsworth Series in Continuing Education

Philip E. Frandson, Consulting Editor
Dean of Extension, University of California, Los Angeles

ARE YOU A TARGET? A GUIDE TO SELF-PROTECTION, PERSONAL SAFETY, AND RAPE PREVENTION by Judith Fein

PCP: THE DEVIL'S DUST—RECOGNITION, MANAGEMENT, AND PREVENTION OF PHENCYCLIDINE ABUSE by Ronald L. Linder, Steven E. Lerner, and R. Stanley Burns

POWER AND CONFLICT IN CONTINUING EDUCATION: SURVIVAL AND PROSPERITY FOR ALL? Sponsored by Wadsworth Publishing Company and The National University Extension Association

Are You a Target?

A Guide to Self-Protection,
Personal Safety, and
Rape Prevention

by Judith Fein, Ph.D.

WADSWORTH PUBLISHING COMPANY

Belmont, California • A Division of Wadsworth, Inc.

Editor: Nancy Taylor
Editing, design, production supervision: Brian K. and Suzanne
Pfeiffer Williams
Interior design: Wendy Cunkle Calmenson
Copyediting: Jeanne Duell and Brian Williams
Photographs: Patricia O'Neil
Line illustrations: Nancy Worthington
Composition: Interactive Composition Corporation

Printed in the United States of America

1 2 3 4 5 6 7 8 9 10—85 84 82 81

Library of Congress Cataloging in Publication Data

Fein, Judith, 1941–
    Are you a target?

    Includes index.
    1. Rape—Prevention.   2. Self-defense for women.
I. Title.
HV6558.F44   362.8'8   80–39606

*This book is dedicated with love
to my parents, Alex and Minnie Fein*

Contents

groin, knee.   Releases and counterattacks.   Multiple assailants.   Knives, guns, tear gas, other weapons.   Home practice.

Preface

This book is about freedom. Its purpose is to help you gain the knowledge, insights, and courage to make the necessary fundamental changes in your life to become a successful assault resister. You are born neither a victim nor a resister. But many of us have become conditioned to behave passively when threatened with physical and/or sexual assault and we agree to become victims.

You don't have to be a victim. Being a resister means that *you* make deliberate choices, *you* make conscious decisions, *you* have control. Being a resister means that, under a given set of circumstances, you decide to do what you believe is in your best interest and determine not to have that power and control taken away from you. This book can show you how. It will provide you with the experiences, background information, and practical tools which will enable you to achieve this end.

Chapter 1 provides you with background on the sociological and psychological aspects of rape. If you are going to fight rape, you need to know what you are fighting. Chapter 2 covers the psychology of self-protection. Here you will learn how the sense of self is so very important in preventing victimization. Chapter 3 focuses on physical defense—practical skills to counter attack or threatened attack. Chapter 4 deals with prevention—with the positive philosophy that if you can prevent as assualt from happening in the first place, you won't have to fight your way out of it. Chapter 5 focuses on the special problems of the career woman. Chapter 6 discusses rape law, rape law reform, and the plight of the rape victim. This chapter by itself may convince you to become a resister.

I believe that women should be free to live their own lives as they choose. It is my hope that *Are You a Target?* will help to guide you in this direction.

Acknowledgments

I would like to express my deepest appreciation to Nancy Worthington for her endless patience, creative insights, and helpful suggestions throughout the many months that this book was being developed. I would like to thank my father, Alex Fein, for his assistance in editing the first drafts of the book. Special thanks go to Patsy O'Neil for her excellent photography and to David Perper for being a good sport in playing the role of villain in the photos. A special note of thanks goes to John Stark, whose article in the *San Francisco Examiner* helped make this book possible, and to Lene Johnson of City College of San Francisco for her encouragement and backing. I would also like to thank my students for providing anecdotal accounts of their experiences and for being in the photographs in this book.

A special acknowledgment: I am deeply grateful to Dr. Jim Selkin of Denver, Colorado, for his pioneering research into the area of rape resistance. His work has helped provide a basic working model from which women can fight back and not succumb to the threat of sexual assault.

Chapter 1

Demystifying Rape

The threat of rape hangs over every female throughout her entire lifetime. The magnitude of this threat is enormous: forcible rape is the fastest growing crime in the United States.[1] The realization that a man can rape a woman and fully expect to get away with it may be startling, but the fact is that no more than 5 percent of reported rape actually results in conviction,[2] and rape has been recognized by law enforcement as one of the most underreported of crimes.[3] Think how many more people would be robbing banks if less than 5 percent of all bank robberies resulted in conviction!

Misconceptions about the nature of rape abound. Though rape is considered to be one of the most heinous crimes, it is often the victim who, instead of feeling righteously angry, is made to feel as if she were the criminal.

Rape Is Not Sex

This confusion arises from the sexual overtones of the crime. But rape involves sex only in that sex is used as the weapon to commit the crime; sex is not its motive.[4] Rape is *violent assault.* If it were thought of in this way, much of the confusion would be dispelled.

Let us see rape for what it really is, so we can clearly understand what we are fighting. The legal definitions are extremely limited. Rape laws have been derived from English common law, and, although each state has its own set of statutes, forcible rape is usually defined as an unconsenting act of sexual intercourse accomplished through force or the threat of force, by a man with a woman who is not the wife of the rapist. Other forms of sexual assault, such as forced oral and anal sex, or the use of objects, are not included in this traditional definition. In marriage, sex performed against the will of the woman is usually not considered rape, probably because, under English common law, intercourse was considered a man's inherent right and a wife was obligated to submit to her husband's demands.

For purposes of this book, then, let us use a more encompassing definition. Rape is *a sexual assault against the will of the victim.*

Why Rapists Rape

Despite American ideals of rugged individualism, truth, and justice, we live in a violent, depersonalized, and mechanized world. Practically every day we hear about crises, some of which could threaten the very existence of the human race. Tensions and frustrations stem from an inability to control our lives.

People tend to take out their frustrations on other people, and they take them out on the ones least able to fight back. If women are thought of in a derogatory way and in addition are unable to fight back, they become likely targets for assault.

The major underlying motive for rape is desire for power and control.[5] Rape is considered an outlet by which men can release their pent-up feelings of powerlessness. One sex offender commented:

As a reformed rapist and a person who has committed violence, I can truthfully say, upon reflection on my past experience, that the aggressive and dominating experiences instilled in me a sense of power. That power was something I did not possess over myself or another person, but, rather something I felt I needed in order to feel part of my environment, a violent and sexist culture which implied power, yet created powerlessness.[6]

Anger is another motive. The rapist uses sex to express anger, hatred, and contempt,[7] venting his rage on his victim in order to retaliate for perceived wrongs or rejections he has suffered at the hands of women. He gains a sense of power and/or satisfaction from degrading and humiliating his victim.

The Rapist

A common stereotype pictures the rapist as a deranged stranger who is unable to control his sexual drive. Lurking in dark alleys or behind hedges, he stalks his prey in the dead of night, brutally ravishing any unfortunate woman who happens to pass by.

The trouble with this stereotype is that it is misleading and can lull one into a false sense of security, unprepared to deal with real potential rape situations. In addition to making you more vulnerable, the lie of this scenario deludes others. To the extent that a rapist doesn't fit the mythical stereotype, his victim's credibility is destroyed and she is not likely to be believed.

Although rapists can be classified in various ways, they broadly fit in two categories: the hostile rapist and the power rapist. The hostile rapist is usually a stranger or one who knows the victim only slightly. There are cases, nevertheless, in which the hostile rapist—a husband, an ex-husband, or a boyfriend—knows or has known the victim intimately. He plans his assault ahead of time, picking out a vulnerable victim. The hostile rapist cannot usually be distinguished from the rest of the male population except that he is more aggressive.[8]

The power rapist usually knows his victim.[9] She may be a date, a relative, a neighbor, an acquaintance, someone who works in the same office, or anyone over whom the attacker has authority. In fact, the overwhelming number of child rapes are committed by relatives or close acquaintances of the child, for whom the rapist is usually an authority figure. The power rapist also usually plans his attack ahead of time, although sometimes he is opportunistic. His psychological characteristics are indistinguishable from the rest of the male population. I was told about a judge attending a convention who asked his legal secretary to come up to his room after dinner to pick up some materials for the next day's meeting. When she arrived, he locked the door, made sexual advances toward her, and warned her against protesting. No one would believe her, he said; he was a judge.

It is estimated that from only half to a twentieth of the total number of rapes are reported.[10] And the closer the relationship between the rapist and the victim, the less likely it is that the police will be notified.[11] Child rapes by family members are usually swept under the rug, and police are extremely reluctant to answer calls when women have been assaulted by their husbands. Yet, over 50 percent of reported rapes are committed by rapists who are acquainted with their victims. [12, 13]

Statistics show that rapists—of either category—are usually young (between fifteen and twenty-three years of age) and have repeatedly committed the crime. They usually choose victims who are similar to them culturally and economically and most often commit the rape in their own neighborhoods.[14]

Nevertheless, I want to emphasize that statistics can be misleading. Rapists attack victims who range in age from babies of six months to adults close to ninety years old. They also cross ethnic and neighborhood boundaries. It is best to remember that the profile of the typical rapist is a composite made from those who have been caught. The rapist can be the average respected member of the community—a coworker in your office, a "helpful" stranger, or your cousin's best friend.

Cultural Conditioning

Clearly, the conditions that lead to rape are deeply rooted in our society. Sex-role stereotypes, for instance, create a climate of acceptance for rape. The mass media, pornography, women's clothes and fashion, even the English language itself all demonstrate ways by which women are subjugated.

Sex-Role Stereotyping

In our society, the deeply ingrained concepts of men's modes of activity and women's modes of activity greatly contribute to the incidence of rape.[15] The polarization of roles from earliest childhood brings about victim behavior on the part of the female and aggressor behavior on the part of the male. (Figure 1.1 is an artistic statement depicting how each sex is trapped into its own polarized role, each the victim of social control.)

"Sugar and spice, and all that's nice" translates as being soft, gentle, self-sacrificing, dependent, and polite. "Snakes and snails

FIGURE 1.1. "Reich's Bull's-eye" by Nancy Worthington. Mixed-media wall relief, 3′9″ × 3′2″ × 2′, 1976. "Every social order produces in the masses of its members that structure which it needs to achieve its main aim."—Wilhelm Reich, *The Mass Psychology of Fascism* (New York: Farrar, Strauss & Giroux, 1970).

and puppy-dogs' tails" means being loud, tough, independent, and adventurous. Girls play hopscotch and tea party and learn it is not nice to get dirty or to be aggressive. Boys play games that teach them competition, strategy, cooperation, independence, and teamwork. Children's books often depict boys in adventurous, physically active roles; girls are often put in the background in unimportant, supportive roles.[16] Boys play at being Superman, junior chemist, or medical doctor. They are told they can become whomever they wish when they grow up—doctors, astronauts, even President of the United States. Girls are often told they can become Mrs. Doctor, Mrs. Astronaut, or even the First Lady. During dating and adolescence these roles are reinforced for women; they learn to need to be taken care of (men take them out), to be weak (men open the door for them), to be dependent (men provide the transportation), to feel obligated (men pay for the dates).

What is the result of this upbringing? A male learns he is supposed to be strong, aggressive, and independent—a competitive breadwinner who makes all the important decisions. A woman learns to believe she needs to be taken care of, to be supported. She wants to be dependent, to be secure, to be accepted by the society, to be considered tactful, gentle, aware of other's feelings. A startling fact is that the typical rape victim has *the same psychological characteristics as the average American woman.*[17] She has become the passive receptor, the acquiescent rape victim, through reinforcement of childhood conditioning.

Thus, in all areas of life, the enforcement and encouragement of sex-role stereotyping conditions women to be weak, vulnerable, and defenseless and men to be aggressive, ruthless, and not sensitive to the rights of others. Rape is an aggressive, ruthless assault characterized by insensitivity to the rights of other human beings.

The Message of the Media

Movies. The movie industry has gone a long way toward perpetuating and encouraging sex-role stereotyping. In sports movies, for example, women either are depicted as sex objects to be used and discarded (as in *North Dallas Forty*) or are so unimportant that they are relegated to the sidelines and not permitted to participate in what is considered the male domain (as in *Breaking Away*). The woman as victim is also a predominant theme (as in Alfred Hitchcock's *Psycho*, in which a woman is brutally murdered). Women who break from tradition and play active, dominant roles are punished; in *Looking for Mr. Goodbar*, for instance, the heroine is raped and murdered for taking the same sexual liberties that men commonly take, and the strong, heroic woman in *Julia* becomes a sacrifice.

Television. Rape-supportive attitudes and myths are constantly reinforced on TV. Women are portrayed as seductive, weak, helpless, and submissive, and the actresses playing these roles are quite often very attractive. Even the Bionic Woman, though strong physically, always made it appear that a man had performed her remarkable feats, and would be shown doing housework bionically or making hamburger patties with incredible speed. (The Bionic Man was never seen cleaning his house or making hamburger patties. He was doing more important things.)

Men are shown as being physically, mentally, and sexually very aggressive. Men on TV are tough; they can fight and take it. A woman threatened with violence, however, is made to appear weak and helpless. The continual presence of violence on the screen, without our having actually to experience the real pain of violence dulls our senses to it. Evening news programs thrive on violence, reporting murders, rapes, and disasters, and the theme of violence is played over and over until it has become the accepted norm rather than the exception.

Advertising. Advertising also reinforces sex-role stereotypes and polarizes men and women. On television, the overwhelming majority of products are endorsed by men. A commercial might show two women in a supermarket discussing a detergent, but it is a male voice from out of nowhere that verifies that the product is good. Evidently, advertisers have decided that men are more credible and authoritative than women.

Advertising also places women in one of the two psychologically accepted roles of women in society: stereotypical roles of Eve, the evil temptress, or the Madonna, the self-sacrificing mother. A perfume ad, for instance, shows a woman as a dutiful, hard-working mother during the day but (after she uses the perfume) as a seductive temptress at night, ready to be ravished by the man who awaits her—a clear reinforcement of the myth that women seduce men and that women secretly wish to be raped. Another common advertisement equates women with objects, especially automobiles; sexy women are used to sell flashy cars. The message is clear: if you buy this object, the car, you will get another object, the woman. Objects are valued differently from human life, of course; they are owned or possessed.

The Culture of Pornography

If, as writers Andra Medea and Kathleen Thompson put it, rape is "all the hatred, contempt, and oppression of women in this society concentrated in one act,"[18] then the flourishing of pornography as an accepted part of our culture is one more thing that conditions people to the acceptance of rape. Books, magazines, movies, record jackets, billboards, even department store windows show women being turned on sexually by being made totally subservient to the male or being degraded for men's pleasure. The mildest, or soft, pornography objectifies women's bodies; women are seen as things rather than as human beings. The worst shows women being bound, gagged, chained, whipped, even tortured or killed. However it is done, soft or hard, pornography degrades women and condones sexual violence toward them, and dehumanizes the relationship between men and women.

The Use of Language

Our language is a vital area in which men are seen as important and women less so. "He" is used to mean "he *or* she." "Man" or "mankind" is used to mean humankind.

In addition, women are constantly thought of—and think of themselves—as girls. A man in a supervisory position will often refer to his secretary (who may be fifty years old) as his "girl." Such paternalistic thinking reduces a woman to the emotional status of a child.

Many slang words also degrade women. If a woman is thought of as a "chick" (baby chicken), "babe" (reducing her to the level of a child), "piece" (of meat?), or "cunt" (reducing her to her sexual organs), she cannot be thought of as a human being. This is the same mentality that impelled American soldiers in Vietnam to refer to the enemy as "gooks." It is more difficult to do violence against someone if you consider that person human, too. A man who respects a woman as a full and equal human being will not rape her.

Clothing

A person's clothing either encourages or restricts movement. It also influences our perception about ourselves and others. Have you ever noticed how practical men's clothing is? The business suit, for example, has many pockets for carrying things and is durable. Men's shoes are made for comfort and made to last. Men's clothes convey a no-nonsense message and lend an aura of credibility and importance to the wearer. Women's clothing, on the other hand, is often very impractical. It has few or no pockets, forcing the woman to carry her valuables in a purse, which is more vulnerable to theft and a hindrance to mobility. Often, she wears high heels or skirts that are too long or too tight and prevent her from being able to flee quickly from a dangerous situation. If she is assaulted, her clothing may be easily ripped off; her skirt gives the assailant easy access. Fashions sometimes make women vulnerable to assault. A woman dressed like a doll looks helpless and naïve; a woman dressed like a seductress looks as though she is signaling her availability.

Six Rape Myths

The attitudes and beliefs that condone rape in our society are sustained by a number of myths. The myths may seem old-fashioned to some, but they still persist in the minds of the general population. These myths blame the victim or diminish her credibility. They vindicate the rapist or justify his acts. Let us contrast these myths with known facts about rape.

Myth One: "Rape Is an Impulsive Act of Passion."

Interpretation.   Men cannot control their sex drives.

Fact.   Rapists themselves do not see rape as compulsive sexual behavior.[19] The motive for rape is not sex, it is power. Sex is used to carry out nonsexual needs.

Myth Two: "Women Want to Be Raped."

Interpretation. Women have fantasies that reflect their desire to be raped.

Fact. Rape is an act of violent aggression. No healthy individual desires to be dehumanized and violated. Any sexual fantasy a woman might have, like any fantasy, is controlled by her.

Myth Three: "Women Ask to Be Raped."

Interpretation. The woman provoked the rape; she tempted the man. ("She should have worn a bra." "Hitchhikers get what they deserve." "She shouldn't have been out so late at night.")

Fact. The blame and responsibility for a criminal assault belong to the assailant, not the victim.

Myth Four: "A Woman Can Run Faster with Her Skirt Up Than a Man Can with His Pants Down."

Interpretation. A woman can't be raped against her will.

Fact. Rape is an aggression committed under force or the threat of force upon an unconsenting person.

Myth Five: "You Can't Blame a Man for Trying."

Interpretation. Responsibility for stopping the man belongs to the woman. Therefore, it's her fault if things get out of hand.

Fact. A criminal, not the victim, is responsible for his acts. Rape is not an impulsive act of passion. It is done for power and control.

Myth Six: "If a Woman Is Going to Be Raped, She Might as Well Relax and Enjoy It."

Interpretation. It's just sex.

Fact. Rape victims experience intense psychological and physical trauma. Rape is a violent, dehumanizing, and intimate invasion of the woman's integrity as a human being. The motive for rape is power; it is not sex. Rape is anything but enjoyable!

Women Can Learn to Fight Back!

Society is slow in changing. Many groups and individuals with a feminist consciousness have begun the enormous task of reeducating everyone—men and women—to the realities of rape and of the need to make changes in our legal, social, and economic processes. If women do not want to be victims of rape, however, they cannot wait for society to change. They must act now to stop rape. In today's world, if a woman is assaulted, she cannot expect or depend on anyone to help or protect her except herself. Victim behavior is learned behavior. Women can make the fundamental changes in themselves that will enable them to prevent, and if necessary counter, an attack on their persons.

Women can stop rape. They can do so by learning psychological and physical skills effectively to *fight back*.

Chapter 2

The Psychology of Self-Protection: Women <u>Can</u> Stop Rape

Women have been told to submit when confronted by a rapist rather than risk the wrath of the assailant. Many have questioned the value of advice that recommends submission to rape. Can one take action instead? Can a woman prevent the assault in the first place? If she cannot prevent an assault, can she counter it? For the most part, the answer to these questions is: *yes*!

Data show that submission does not result in significantly less physical violence than fighting back, as was once thought. If you submit, he may beat you up anyway

No matter how small or how old the woman is, or how big or how strong the rapist, a woman can prevent and effectively resist assault. I have taught children, grandmothers in their sixties, and women who are physically handicapped. Colleen M., a blind woman who has taken my self-defense course, relates her experiences:

Women Do Not Have to Be Victims

Several years ago when I was eighteen years old I was beaten and raped in Los Angeles. I know blind women who have been raped and are hassled a lot. Being blind is an open invitation to an attacker. After being raped, I went through a lot of hellish turmoil. When I moved to northern California to go to college, I began a course in self-defense for women. I began to think about rape objectively and the effect the experience has had on my life. Instead of feeling so terribly vulnerable, I realized that I could reduce the chances of rape attack by awareness and body language. I began to work with the psychological and physical tools of rape prevention. I began to know that I had control over my life. Recently, I had occasion to use some of the techniques which I learned. Several men came up to me, separated me from my German Shepherd guide dog, and tried to assault me. I got angry, yelled "leave me alone," sent out bad vibes, and kicked at them. I was not assaulted.

The Sense of Self

The psychology of self-protection starts with a fundamental belief in your own worth as a human being. As I've mentioned, women have been taught from childhood to be dependent, fragile, submissive, passive, and to think negatively about themselves. They have been conditioned to believe that they do not have the power to determine their own values, needs, actions, or thoughts. If women are to stop being rape victims, they must rethink and fundamentally change the way they feel about themselves and the way they perceive society. A woman must learn to like herself and nurture a belief in her ability to change and grow. Developing a positive identity, she will come to see herself as special and important—and regard what she does as having value. In essence, a woman develops a positive sense of self. It is this sense of self, this self-respect, that is psychologically so essential in preventing rape. Whether or not a woman has been a rape victim in the past, she can make the necessary changes in her life so that no rape will occur in the future.

Minimizing

To prevent rape, a woman has to think in terms of reducing her vulnerability. A rapist selects a vulnerable target.[1] An assailant certainly would not choose Wonder Woman as his prey; she would pick him up and hurl him across the room. A rapist chooses a woman who is vulnerable to attack. She may be old, or young, or handicapped; she may look particularly weak or fragile. He finds a victim who is unaware (Figure 2.1) or whose mental state prevents her from reacting appropriately or swiftly to the threat of rape. Thus, he may prey upon depressed women, or women who are on drugs or intoxicated. In Denver, between 1970 and 1972, almost

FIGURE 2.1.   Rapists often look
for victims who are unaware.

one-fourth of the victims of sexual assault were under the influence
of drugs or alcohol at the time of attack.[2] A rapist may also look for a
victim in an isolated environment (Figure 2.2). If the victim is a
hitchhiker, for example, or if she is alone with the rapist in her
home, she is particularly vulnerable. In order to minimize the
chances of being assaulted, you must take awareness, body language, and personal safety and physical security precautions into
account. These are all methods of reducing the risk of being
targeted as a rape victim.

Practicing Prevention

The concept of prevention refers to avoiding dangerous situations. A woman needs to be aware of her environment and of situations that can lead to rape. By being conscious of these factors, she
can act on her knowledge and prevent potentially dangerous situations from occurring. Prevention encompasses measures for both

FIGURE 2.2. Rapists look for victims in isolated environments. (Photo by J. R. Hendrickson.)

physical security and personal safety. This concept is vitally important. If a woman can prevent a situation from occurring in the first place, she is not put in a position of having to fight her way out of it. Some typical questions I am asked are:

- What do I do if I am driving my car and a man who has been hiding in the back seat puts a knife to my throat?
- What do I do if my date takes me to his apartment and wants to have sex with me against my will?
- What do I do if I wake up in the middle of the night and a man is standing over my bed?

These can be very difficult situations to get out of. Actions can be taken to counter these circumstances, but they are not without potential danger. Therefore, my answer to these questions is that the best thing to do is to think in terms of prevention.

- You can take steps to prevent the man from being able to get into your car (see Chapter 4).

- If you did not know your date well enough to trust him, it would have been better not to go to his apartment at all. (Prevention of rapes by acquaintances is discussed later in this chapter.)

- Physical security measures can prevent someone from entering your home in the middle of the night without your knowledge (see Chapter 4).

If a woman reaches old age without having been assaulted or robbed, it is not because of luck. It is because she has kept distance between herself and potential assailants. She has practiced prevention. Specific personal safety and physical security measures and self-defense will be discussed in later chapters.

Body Language as Warning

In all your gestures and movements—when you walk down the street or come into contact with someone—you are sending out specific nonverbal messages. Unconsciously, your body telegraphs your thoughts, feelings, and perceptions. It tells others how you feel about yourself, how you perceive them, and how you are responding to a situation.[3] You can transmit signals that say "I am a strong person, I respect myself," or you can say, nonverbally, "I am afraid."

Several years ago, a woman visiting me noticed my Siamese cat, Peter, lying comfortably on the couch. She was afraid of cats, and subconsciously her body language telegraphed this message. Peter was a very congenial and gentle fellow, almost always purring. He had never attacked anyone in his life, but without warning he ran over and bit my guest on the leg. Animals read body language and react. So does an assailant.

Use of body language is an integral aspect of self-defense and rape prevention. Proper use can effectively ward off a potential assailant, conveying the message "I am alert, I am aware, I am not a weak vulnerable victim. Don't mess with me!"

It is not necessary constantly to send out "Don't mess with me" signals. This would require a tremendous, steady expenditure of energy. A strong "Don't mess with me" signal implies determined anger and the intention to follow through on your anger and to fight if necessary. In rape prevention, your body language conveys messages on two basic levels.

First Level: Radar. You are aware of your environment. The messages that you transmit state that you respect yourself, that you have confidence in yourself, that you are alert, and that you are not vulnerable to attack. Your posture is erect, your head is held high. Your vision is directed forward. You walk briskly and with confidence (see also Chapters 3 and 4). (Figure 2.3 depicts an alert individual in the foreground. The individual in the background seems unaware of her environment.)

Once you have made the necessary changes in your life and have developed a consciousness of rape prevention, this level of awareness will become an everyday habit, a part of your personality.

If your personal territory is invaded, if you are approached by a potential assailant, or if you are in an especially dangerous envi-

FIGURE 2.3. Alert and not alert individuals.

ronment, your level of awareness and preparedness instantly magnifies to the second level.

Second Level: Full Alert. One of my evening classes is held in a college gymnasium, necessitating a walk from the parking lot. The area is poorly lighted and virtually deserted at that hour. Instead of fearing that someone is going to jump me from behind a bush, I send out very strong signals. I am acutely aware of my potentially dangerous environment, and my body language clearly states, "No one had better come near me, or if he does, he's going to be very sorry he got out of bed this morning!" This, clearly, is the "Don't mess with me" signal (see also Chapter 3).

"Don't mess with me" signals can include verbal as well as body language. Betty, a student in my defense against rape course, recounts:

I was jogging down a street near where I live, and a young punk approached me and said he was going to smash my face in. I got angry and began sending out vicious signals. I yelled, "You'd better not try to lay a hand on me!" He was really knocked back with my outburst. He dropped the brick he was carrying, crossed the street, and proceeded on his way in the opposite direction.

Preventing Sexual Assault by Acquaintances

As I discussed in the preceding chapter, the majority of rapists are known by their victims.[4] They are, for the most part, not considered sick, and have the same psychological characteristics as the *man next door*.[5] Most rapes take place indoors[6] and are planned ahead of time.[7]

Teenagers are particularly vulnerable to rape by acquaintances, and often an adolescent is the victim of more than one attacker at a time. Frequently, the rape occurs during social occasions such as parties. Typically, the young woman is seeking friendship and peer acceptance and gets into a situation beyond her control.

Jill relates an incident that took place many years before but is still vivid in her mind:

I was a freshman in college, and I was invited to a football game and fraternity party by a senior. He suggested we leave the game early and go to the party, which he said was already in progress. I sensed something was wrong but didn't say anything because I didn't think he would lie to me and didn't want to appear naïve. He took me to his fraternity house, which was way out in the country. No one else was there. . . .

Preventing Entrapment

Preventing the familiar rape has a lot to do with the concept of respect, the respect the other person has for you and the respect you have for yourself. It involves a strong sense of self, awareness, and avoidance of situations leading to entrapment, and it involves using and acting upon your intuition.

The Concept of Respect. The acquaintance whose intent is rape does not respect you as a full and equal human being. When two people respect each other, rape does not occur. The rapist will consider you to be less of a person than he is—an object or someone he intends to vanquish. The game is to manipulate you into a trap, and the goal of the game is to score.

If you respect yourself and believe in your worth as a human being, you have the power to determine the course of your life, to make your own decisions, and to be free from the absolute authority of others. You will not permit yourself to be manipulated into a situation that you feel is a trap. You are your own person.

Use Your Intuition. Nobody knows you better than yourself. If you sense that something is wrong in a situation, it is! Suppose a man in your office suggests that you stop for a drink after work. You tell him that you can't this particular evening. He still tries to convince you. You feel uneasy. When an alarm goes off in your mind telling you that something is not exactly right, then something *is not exactly right.* Learn to listen to your feelings and act on them. If someone pushes just a little too hard, doesn't seem to respect your wishes or feelings, treats you more like an object than a person, or seems to bear a grudge against you, stay clear. This concept of trusting your intuition is backed by a study in rape prevention and resistance conducted by the Queen's Bench Foundation in San Francisco. The Queen's Bench found that women who avoided being raped were more likely than victims to trust feelings of suspicion, even though they didn't know why they felt uneasy. [8]

Often it may seem difficult to avoid entrapment when the man is someone you respect or in a position of authority, or is someone with whom you want to be on good terms but whom you do not know very well. Suppose a college professor asks you to meet him in his office that evening to discuss your progress in his class. You may feel uncomfortable about the situation, but if you ignore your inner warnings because you don't want to look foolish or offend him, you may be maneuvered into a trap. If you think that you can outsmart him, you might be wrong, for he may have played the game before and indeed be a highly skilled player.

Be Wary of Friends' Friends.   One acquaintance to be guarded about is the friend of a friend or of a relative. When you are introduced to such a person, you may be inclined to accord him the same degree of familiarity with which you would treat your friend. ("Any friend of yours is a friend of mine.") You are advised to be cautious and stay out of isolated or unusual situations with this person.

Avoid Double Messages.   In communicating to another person, make sure that your verbal and nonverbal messages don't contradict each other. If you say "No," your body language (posture, gestures, eye contact) and your tone of voice must also say "No." Your refusal must be clear or it may be misinterpreted.

Avoid Entrapment.   Once you begin to play the trapper's game, you will have an uphill battle. The way to prevent entrapment, then, is to refuse to play the game at all. Assert yourself, be blunt even. Don't feel you need to apologize or make excuses. If he is being honest, he won't be offended.

Your objective is to prevent an assault from happening in the first place, through personal safety precautions and physical security measures.

Even though you may have taken all possible precautions to prevent an assault, there are times when threats to your person may occur. Here your aim is to get away safely. This does not mean submitting to rape or degrading yourself (by pleading or vomiting, for instance). Pleading or trying to talk him out of it by being understanding are not effective deterrents.[9] Telling the rapist you are

Countering Assault by Strangers

flattered by his attention and then later trying to kick him in the genitals may invite severe retaliation.[10] The longer you wait, the longer the rapist has to consolidate his control over you.

Surrender or Resist?

When confronted by a rapist, you have two options: You can surrender or you can resist. The decision is yours. If you submit, the very least that will happen is that you will be raped. That is, you will suffer an extremely traumatizing attack, the physical and psychological effects of which may last your entire life. Under most circumstances, if you follow the principles of resistance described in this chapter and in Chapter 3, you will have your best chance to escape unharmed.

If you submit, the rapist takes away your control and can do anything he wants—beat you, rape you repeatedly, perform sadistic acts.

Victims versus Resisters. There are definite behavioral differences between rape victims and rape resisters. Victims, Selkin found, experienced emotions akin to physical and mental paralysis when confronted by assailants. They experienced shock and terror, froze, panicked, and behaved submissively during the assault. Resisters, on the other hand, felt rage and anger, and their emotional state provoked outcry and action, as a result of which they were not raped. Resisters were found to be more confident and assertive than victims.[11]

These differences are demonstrated by two women under similar circumstances. The first woman was working alone in a small shop when, at closing time, with no customers in the shop, a man walked in and handed her a card that read, "I have a gun. Do not make a sound. Come into the back room with me and do as I say or I will kill you." Paralyzed with fear, the woman meekly went into the back room and was raped. The second woman was at work in the shop when, several weeks later, the man returned near closing time and approached with the same card. The woman read the card and became incensed. "You have some nerve coming in here!" she yelled. "You goddamned bastard, get the hell out of here!" Taken aback, the would-be assailant fled.

The woman who was raped suffered serious psychological

trauma and experienced such severe anxiety, nightmares, and depression that after a year she left the country.

Threat with a Weapon.   If an assailant claims to have a lethal weapon, calmly ask to see it. While this may seem unthinkable at first, the fact is that many women are raped by men who intimidate them with nonexistent weapons. According to Amir, the assailant actually displayed a dangerous weapon in no more than 20 percent of the cases he studied.[12] Think of that: in 80 percent of such cases, there was no weapon involved!

If an assailant produces or threatens you with a weapon, it need not necessarily mean he has rape in mind. Try to ascertain if robbery is the motive; if so, it may be best to cooperate. Property can be replaced, you cannot. However, in no way should you permit the assailant to intimidate you. A rapist will often rob his victim before he rapes her in order to test the victim's "willingness to submit herself to his will."[13]

If you suspect the assailant intends to kill you or if he tries to take you to an isolated area, then you should resist. Bart, in a study of rape avoidance, found that the presence of a weapon was not the main factor differentiating rape from rape avoidance.[14] The major concern of the women who avoided rape was "the concern with not being raped rather than the fear of death and/or mutilation."[15] An example of the price of nonresistance can be seen in the case of Chicago mass murderer Richard Speck: Seven of his victims allowed Speck to gag them without resisting; indeed, they did not make a sound as he slashed their throats. The weight of clinical evidence, according to Selkin, "is that the murder-rape victim sets out to cooperate with her assailant. The rapist's need to murder is stimulated and provoked by elements within him and elements at the scene of the crime. He murders to satisfy his own inner need in an environment where he feels that he can *safely act out these needs* [emphasis mine]."[16]

Choosing Not to Fight Back.   Under certain circumstances, it may *not* be in your best interest to resist or immediately resist, and you might choose other alternatives. It is important that *you choose* whether to fight back or not; *you* must remain in control over what you will or will not do. Under no circumstances should you panic or permit the assailant to intimidate you. If you decide not to resist immediately and vigorously, remain calm and in control, evaluate the situation, and see what your options are. You may, for example, decide to wait for the rapist to make a mistake and then make your move. Or if fighting back is out of the question (because you are being attacked by a gang with weapons, say) and you decide not to resist, try to remember as much as you can about your assailants to aid in their apprehension later (see Chapter 6). Whatever decision you make, in no case should you feel guilty about it; after all, you are doing the best you can under the circumstances.

Fear of Fighting

"We have been trained to cry, to wheedle, to plead, to look for a male protector," observes Susan Brownmiller, "but we have never been trained to fight and win."[17] "The ideal woman," adds Phyllis Chesler, "avoids committing direct physical violence—and avoids her own self-preservation. . . . Traditionally, the ideal female is trained to *lose* and the ideal male is trained to *win*."[18]

As a result of societal conditioning and taboos, then, combined with a dismal lack of physical training in vigorous competitive athletic or fighting skills, women in general have fears about fighting back. Since most have never struck anyone, they may be afraid of their own inability to hurt or incapacitate anyone. They may be uneasy about their own anger, or afraid that the assailant will get angry. Indeed, they even may not wish to hurt the assailant (albeit at what cost to themselves?).

It is important to realize, however, that *in order to stop someone who is attacking you, you indeed have to hurt him.* You must, in fact, *incapacitate* him so that he cannot come after you.

Self-Defense Training

One means by which women can combat their passivity and helplessness is to undertake self-defense training, which combines both psychological and physical skills. When taught from a feminist perspective, self-defense training gives women the confidence, knowledge, and ability to make the changes in themselves necessary to prevent and counter threats to their person (Figure 2.4). Brownmiller, in her book *Against Our Will*, recounts her own self-defense training:

How strange it was to hear for the first time in my life that women could fight back, should fight back . . . that it is in our interest to know how to

FIGURE 2.4. Self-defense training.

do it. . . . We women discovered in wonderment that as we learned to place our kicks and jabs with precision we were actually able to inspire fear in the men. . . . Fighting back. On a multiplicity of levels, that is the activity we must engage in . . . if we—women—are able to redress the imbalance and rid ourselves and men of the ideology of rape.[19]

Anger as a Weapon

The rapist does not expect to encounter anger in his victim. Rather, he expects her to be fearful, to be intimidated, and to submit. In our culture, it is acceptable for a man to get angry, but for a woman it is considered "unfeminine" or crazy. Traditionally, women have not been permitted to express anger overtly.

Thus, it is crucial when you are approached by an assailant intent on intimidation that you immediately get in touch with your anger.

Think, "How dare he try to hurt me! How dare he try to invade my personal territory and control me in such an intimate and degrading way!" A woman who knows her own feelings and who respects her own integrity also knows that it is *right* to become angry and outraged and does not let the anger turn inward later in the form of guilt and depression. She accepts the anger and, like a powerful shock wave or force field, with sound and fury directs it at the rapist. This anger, combined with the readiness to support it physically if necessary, will tell the assailant in no uncertain terms, to "Back off!" (see Figure 2.5).

I had occasion to put this principle to work for myself recently. I was taking photographs at an art festival one Sunday afternoon. While checking the reading on my light meter, I sensed something was wrong and looked up to find five men quickly closing in on me.

"Hey," one of them called out, "is that light meter expensive?"

"Move out of the way," I replied. "I'm trying to take pictures."

Instead, the circle closed even tighter and a man grabbed at the meter, which was on a strap around my neck. I was outraged: How dare he try to grab something right off of me! Immediately I got

FIGURE 2.5. Anger used to push assailant back.

into my karate stance. "Get out of here!" I yelled, directing a wave of anger at him, simultaneously delivering a well-placed kick. The circle melted and the men scattered.

Yelling

Yelling is a potent weapon in rape prevention. In an analysis of thirty-six uncompleted and thirty-six completed rapes, Javorek found that 69 percent of the women who screamed (and 75 percent who ran) escaped being raped.[20] All of us are afraid of loud, unexpected sounds. Moreover, your yelling may attract attention, and an assailant certainly doesn't want an audience. A loud, blood-curdling battle cry will disorient the rapist and help get your adrenaline going. If you feel inhibited about yelling, practice.

Stopping a Stranger Rape Assault

In analyzing the behavior patterns of stranger rapists,[21] Selkin found that rapists follow predictable patterns. Thus, if you are aware of their methods of operation, you can prevent or, if necessary, successfully resist assault. The first pattern is that potential rapists target their victims; they look for women who appear vulnerable to assault. A rapist then approaches his victim and tests her to see if she can be intimidated. He may very well threaten to kill her. The rapist may be hostile, abusive, hateful, and threatening, may make lewd or insinuating remarks, and may grab, hit, or rob.

As in the method for preventing the rape by a familiar person, an awareness of the rapist's psychology is important. He is testing to see whether or not his victim can be intimidated. This testing phase is crucial for the rapist because *if he cannot intimidate the victim, he will not rape her*. Because he needs ordered, controlled behavior from his victim, needs her to be immobilized with fear, he will tell her or threaten her with anything in order to gain her cooperation and submission. As Brownmiller puts it, "A quid pro quo—rape in exchange for life or rape in exchange for a good-faith guarantee against hurtful or disfiguring damage—dominates the female mentality in rape."[22] Remember that once you are under the rapist's control he can do *anything* he wants to you in addition to raping you.

The *key* to breaking up a rape assault is *immediate resistance* and an *absolute refusal to be intimidated*. Instead of becoming paralyzed with fear, you need to respond with anger. You need to send out all the outrage and wrath that you can muster, the anger that has built up inside of you through your entire lifetime. Let out a loud yell. Attack if necessary to incapacitate the assailant. And run.

Eve O., a student in one of my self-defense courses, tells how expressing her rage worked for her:

I was on my way home after jogging. Suddenly, a hand went over my mouth and the weight of a man's body forced me face down into the dirt. He threatened to kill me unless I obeyed him. A knife was held at my throat. Through visions of death, I could have fainted then, but I didn't. I became outraged by the thought of this person threatening my life. Through my surge of anger came a burst of strength and when I was sure the knife was no longer over me, I fought with all my might. This man was determined to rape and, I felt, to kill me. I had made up my mind he was not going to. I don't think he was expecting a hard time, and when he found that he wasn't going to get what he wanted he ran.

The man was experienced. It turned out he was a parolee from prison on prior charges arising from sexual assault. During the brief five-week period since his release from prison, he had attacked six women. I was the only one he had not raped.

Key Points to Remember

1. Self-protection begins with a strong sense of self: self-respect and the fundamental belief in your worth as a human being.
2. Self-defense training, combining both physical and psychological skills, and taught from a feminist perspective, gives women the confidence, knowledge, and ability to prevent and to counter rape assaults.
3. Practice measures of prevention. Through physical security and personal safety measures, you can avoid danger and prevent dangerous situations from occurring.
4. Use body language to ward off potential assailants. As a first level of awareness, send out messages indicating alertness, self-confidence, and self-respect. If approached by a potential assailant, magnify your level of awareness to *full alert* and send out *don't mess with me* signals.
5. Prevent entrapment. Be aware of and avoid compromising situations. Heed your intuitions and act upon them.
6. Minimize vulnerability. Rapists look for women who are vulnerable to attack. Women in isolated environments, women

who look weak or fragile, and woman who cannot react swiftly or appropriately are especially vulnerable.

7. If you are faced with physical assault, your objective is to get away safely. Absolutely refuse to be intimidated. Under most circumstances, your best option is to resist immediately and vigorously. Get in touch with your anger and direct this anger at the rapist. Yell. Attack if necessary; incapacitate the assailant. Run.

8. Victims and resisters behave differently under threat of assault. Victims become terrified, panicked, and frozen, and submit to the rapist. Resisters become angry and outraged. They yell and take physical action to escape being raped.

Chapter 3

Techniques of Physical Self-Defense: Learning to Fight Back

Despite all precautions, there may be circumstances in which you may be assaulted or threatened with rape. This is a crisis situation that threatens both your physical safety and your integrity as a human being. The principles and skills described in this chapter provide you with appropriate responses for such a crisis. Remember: You have the legal and moral right to fight back.

In California, the laws of self-defense state that if a person is being assaulted or if as a reasonable person believes that bodily injury is *about* to be inflicted, it is lawful to defend herself or himself. The victim may use all the force that she or he believes is reasonably necessary to prevent injury (and that would appear so to a reasonable person in the same or similar circumstances). California laws are fairly representative of most state laws.

If attacked or threatened with attack, you need to be able to respond by immediately incapacitating the assailant. If he's just a little hurt, he can still come after you. The longer you fight, the less chance you will have of escaping unhurt. Remember, there is absolutely *no* sportsmanship involved. You are fighting for your safety, your well-being, your integrity—and possibly your life. Don't feel sorry for the rapist, and don't be afraid to use full force because you may hurt him. You did not start the fight, he did. Go all out and at once!

Eight Rules of Fighting

The techniques covered below, combining karate and street fighting, will enable you to incapacitate an attacker quickly and escape. Unlike the martial arts, these are relatively simple skills that can be learned in a short time. Once learned, however, they must be practiced regularly until they become second nature. Fighting back effectively is a learned and trained response.

1. Fight to Win

When you make the decision to fight back, do so with the full commitment to win. Anything less diminishes your effectiveness. If you think you are going to lose, you probably will. You must not struggle ineffectively or make a halfhearted attempt to fight back. If you hurt your assailant slightly but not enough to stop him, he will become even angrier. When you incapacitate him, no matter how angry he is, he cannot come after you.

2. When Attacked or Threatened with Attack, Immediately Resist

The rapist does not expect you to fight back. He expects a passive, frightened, submissive victim. The longer you wait to resist, the better opportunity you give the rapist psychologically and physically to intimidate you into submission. In most cases, the key is immediate and forceful resistance, starting with surprise and taking advantage of the attacker's disorientation by quickly incapacitating him. (However, you must consider each situation carefully. If the assailant has a gun or if there are many attackers, you may choose to modify your defense; see Chapter 2.)

3. Yell—Loudly

As mentioned, yelling is an important weapon. Since we are all afraid of loud, unexpected sounds, the yell will disorient the assailant and, in addition, possibly attract attention. Yelling will also help you physically and psychologically to be more aggressive. It opens your breathing and brings more oxygen to your muscles. Make sure that your yell is a loud, vicious battle cry that rises from your diaphragm and is directed at the assailant. Take a deep breath, open your mouth, look mean and vicious, and yell, "Yaaah!" Yell every single time you punch, kick, block, break from a hold, and counterattack.

4. Attack Vulnerable Areas

It doesn't matter how big or strong the assailant is. He will be seriously disabled if attacked in vulnerable areas. Therefore, they are your target. It does you more harm than good merely to hurt the attacker. Kicking him in the shin takes time and does not stop him. Kicking him in the kneecap does stop him. Vulnerable areas are shown in Figure 3.1. The body has many vital spots; of these it is best to concentrate on several that you can strike quickly in suc-

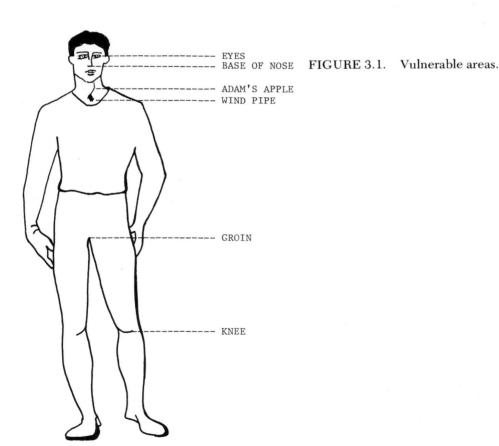

EYES
BASE OF NOSE
ADAM'S APPLE
WIND PIPE
GROIN
KNEE

FIGURE 3.1.   Vulnerable areas.

cession and that are easily accessible. Aim your attacks *through* the following target areas: *eyes, nose, neck, groin,* and *knee*.

5. Maintain Eye Contact

Look directly into the assailant's eyes in order to intimidate him. In addition, the eye contact will prevent you from looking at the area you are about to strike, which telegraphs your moves.

6. Direct Your Anger

When you are fighting or confronting the assailant, you should send out a force field of anger. Your body language should tell the attacker unequivocally that you mean business. You are communicating to him that you are angry, outraged, furious. Look directly into his eyes with an intimidating "drop dead" glare; snarl, flare your nostrils, and move toward him, pushing him back. Direct toward him all the anger that has been building inside of you during your entire lifetime. He will quickly get the message that he picked the wrong person to attack and that he had better try to leave as fast as he can.

7. Use the Correct Principles in Fighting

Utilize the principles of force, stability, distance, and speed. Contributing to an effective attack and defense, they may make the difference between winning and losing. (These principles will be explained in conjunction with the basic skills below.)

8. Be Flexible.

Analyze the situation to determine which vulnerable areas are reachable and how to deliver your attack most effectively. If one defense or attack isn't effective, try another. Learn the basic skills of fighting and apply them to the specific situation.

Basic Skills

In order to fight most effectively, you must become skilled in basic techniques. You should learn and repeatedly practice fundamental fighting skills until they become automatic. You can then be free to concentrate on dealing with the situation rather than worrying about your body position.

The Fighting Stance

Psychologically, your correct stance sends out the positive message that you know what you are doing (see Figure 3.2). When a potential assailant tries to intimidate you, immediately assume your stance and deliver verbal and nonverbal "Don't mess with me" signals.

Physically, you fight from the stance. Every single fighting technique starts from the stance (or modified stance). You get into the stance as you are responding to the attack. The stance provides stability and power. The lower you are to the ground and the wider your base of support (your legs), the more balanced and stable you are. Much of your power comes from your legs, which must be bent in order to maximize this force. A punch from a standing position is a lot weaker. The stance is an ideal position from which to maneuver for attack and defense.

FIGURE 3.2. The basic fighting stance: front view and side view.

Here's how to get into the stance:

1. Stand with your left side (if you are right-handed) to the assailant. This will present the smallest target to the person you are fighting.
2. Place your legs a comfortable distance apart (one foot to two feet), pointing your left foot at the assailant.
3. Bend your arms at the elbows, holding them a little away from your body.
4. Hold your rear hand palm up, your front hand turned so that the thumb is on top, and your fingers and thumbs slightly bent and together.
5. Bend your knees so that you are "sitting" into the stance. Point your head in the direction of the assailant and look directly into his eyes. Keep your torso erect and your body balanced on the balls of both feet.

The Punch

The clenched-fist punch is one of the very first skills to master because, as you learn to punch, you learn how to utilize force and power—principles that must be employed in every attack or defense.

Making the Fist
1. Extend an arm in front of you, palm down. Curl your thumb on the outside of your fist so that it is on top of and supporting your first two fingers (see Figure 3.3).
2. In punching, concentrate your force on the upper knuckles of these two fingers.
3. Keep your wrist tight and straight. Without a tight fist, your blows will be weak and you may injure your wrist or hand.

Arm Coordination
1. Start in the basic stance.
2. Clench your fists.
3. Wind up by bringing your right elbow straight back, palm up, so that your upper arm is parallel to the floor.
4. Attack! Aim at the assailant's Adam's apple. Thrust your arm forward, turning it so that, upon impact, it is palm down. The

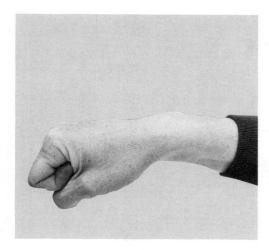

FIGURE 3.3.   The clenched fist.

front arm acts in opposition to the rear arm. At the same time
the rear arm thrusts forward, the front arm moves back to the
side, bent at the elbow, palm up. Your arms are then ready
for the second punch.

Delivering the Punch
1. First wind up for the punch (Figure 3.4a).
2. Yell.
3. At the same time you start to punch, raise your rear heel and
   pivot counterclockwise on the ball of this foot, thrusting
   down and back so that you practically straighten your rear leg
   (Figure 3.4b).
4. Swing your right hip forward, squaring off your shoulders.
   Keep your left knee bent and your torso erect. Do not lean
   forward. Your weight remains evenly distributed on both
   legs.
5. Your right arm should now be thrust forward, palm down,
   and your left arm should be at your side, bent at the elbow,
   palm up and ready for the second punch.
6. Punch decisively.
7. To punch a second time, immediately wind up the left arm,
   and, without losing momentum, punch as fast and as forcefully as possible. Your feet remain in the forward thrust position that you just completed in the first punch.

FIGURE 3.4. The punch. (a) The wind-up. (b) The delivery.

Kicking

Kicking may be your best attack, for several reasons—particularly surprise. In the United States, kicking is just not expected. A second reason for kicking is force. Because your legs are stronger than your arms, you can kick harder than you can punch. A third reason is that your legs are longer than your assailant's arms, so you can kick him from beyond the range of his arms. Fourth, if you kick low (aiming in most cases at the kneecap), your kick is hard to block. It is for all these reasons that I recommend kicking whenever possible.

Front Snap Kick

1. Start from the stance. (If you don't have time to assume your stance before you kick or if it would ruin the element of surprise, get into it *as* you kick.)
2. Using your back leg, raise your knee so that it is straight out in front of you, as shown in Figure 3.5a. (The height of the knee depends upon the height of the kick. Raise your knee higher for a high kick and lower for a low kick.)
3. At the same time you are lifting your knee, flex your ankle upward and curl your toes upward.
4. Snap the foot straight forward, aiming at the assailant's kneecap and making contact with the ball of your foot (Figure 3.5b).
5. Immediately retract your foot so it cannot be grabbed, and then bring your leg back down into the stance (Figure 3.5 c). Bring your leg either forward or backward into the stance, depending upon your adjustment for distance (to be discussed later in this chapter).
6. If you have trouble balancing, lean forward slightly and bend at the waist.
7. Your kick should be made forcefully and quickly, in one continuous motion, without hesitation and without telegraphing your attack. Always be sure to yell.

The Side Kick. This kick is used when you want to attack someone positioned at your side. The side kick has a greater range than the snap kick. Kick with the leg that is closest to the assailant.

FIGURE 3.5. The front snap kick. (a) Raising knee. (b) Snapping the foot straight forward, aiming at assailant's kneecap with ball of foot. (c) Retracting the leg into the fighting stance.

1. To kick with your right leg, put your weight on your left foot, drop your left shoulder, and lift your right knee. Again, the height to which you raise your knee depends upon the height of the target you are kicking. (Figure 3.6a).
2. Kick to the side, making contact with the heel or ball of the foot. Depending upon the position of the assailant, your side kick should be aimed at his kneecap or at the side of his knee (Figure 3.6b).
3. Immediately retract your leg and return to the starting position (Figure 3.6c).

The Back Kick. This kick is similar to the side kick: Pivot to the side, then kick as you would in a side kick (Figure 3.7).

Blocking

Blocking is crucial to your defense. It is a means of deflecting an attack to prevent it from reaching you. The principles of blocking are as follows:

1. *Move back on the block.* If someone is attacking you, it is best for you to move away from the direction of the attack. Moving back will (a) lessen the impact of the attack, (b) possibly throw the assailant off balance, and (c) give you more time to respond to the attack.
2. *Use full force in executing a block.* You need maximum power to divert a forceful attack. To maximize power wind up, take your stance, clench your fists, and block quickly.
3. *Block away from your body, not toward it.* Aim the direction of your block away from your body area. If the attack is aimed at or toward your right side, block with your right arm; if the attack is aimed at or toward your left side, block with your left arm. Suppose, for example, the assailant has a broken bottle and swings it across your body in the direction of your left shoulder. If you use your right arm to block, rather than your left, you will bring the bottle across your face.
4. *Block to protect a specific zone.* In most ball games you strike a specific object; when you block, however, you protect a specific area of your body. If you bat at the assailant's arm, you protect only a small area, perhaps only as wide as your fist. Consequently, you must block to protect an entire zone without attempting to strike directly at the assailant's arm. In

FIGURE 3.6. The side kick. (a) Launching the kick. (b) The kick, aimed at assailant's kneecap. (c) Retracting the leg.

a

b

c

FIGURE 3.7.   The back kick.

so doing, you will cover a greater area, and the assailant's arm will be deflected so that it does not reach you.

5. *Stop the block just beyond your body area.* It is counterproductive to follow through on the block. Swinging your arm out of line will carry you off balance and prevent you from making an immediate counterattack. Make sure, however, to complete the block and not stop short.

Let us now consider three kinds of specific blocks.

The Downward Block. Executed with the outer surface of the forearm, this block is used to deflect attacks directed toward your lower body. Use either your right or left arm, depending upon the direction of the attack.

1. From your stance, with your fist clenched, wind up by placing your arm upward across your body so that your fist is facing and almost touching the opposite shoulder (Figure 3.8a).
2. Forcefully swing your arm diagonally downward—yelling as you do so—crossing your body, stopping directly next to the

FIGURE 3.8. The downward block. (a) The wind-up. (b) The block. (c) Correct arm position blocking assailant's attack.

a

outside of the thigh, fist facing inward. The elbow remains slightly bent, and the distance between the fist and the thigh is about six inches (Figure 3.8b).

3. Make contact with the assailant's arm, between his elbow and wrist (Figure 3.8c).
4. Remember to move back as you block. To do this, step back with your back foot first, then your front foot. Take small, quick steps.

Do not turn your back on the assailant. Coordinate the movement of the back foot with the windup and the front foot with the downward movement of the block.

The Upward Block. This block is used to deflect an attack aimed at your waist or above.

1. Wind up by placing your arm downward across your body, fist clenched, palm facing inward, so that your fist is opposite your hip, as if you were going to draw a sword out of its sheath (Figure 3.9a).

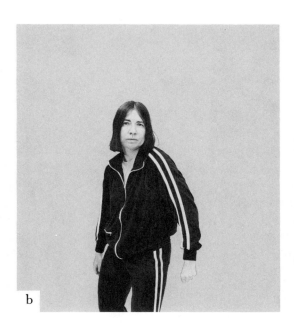

b

c

FIGURE 3.9. The upward block. (a) The wind-up, with arm down across body. (b) The block itself, with arm swung upward across the body. (c) Correct arm position blocking assailant's attack.

a

b

c

2. With your elbow bent, swing your arm diagonally upward and outward across your body. The arc of this swing passes across your nose and stops directly opposite the temple (Figure 3.9b). Your palm will be facing inward, your upper arm parallel to the floor, and your forearm perpendicular to the floor. (The elbow will be at a right angle, and you will be in a "making a muscle" position.) Make contact with the assailant's arm between his elbow and wrist (Figure 3.9c).

The Upward X-Block. This block is used to deflect an attack made with a stick or club aimed downward at your head.

1. From the stance, cross both fists at the wrists in front of your body (Figure 3.10a).
2. Extend both arms over your head, with your palms facing outward (Figure 3.10b).

a   b

FIGURE 3.10. The upward X-block, to deflect attack with stick. (a) Starting stance, with arms crossed at wrists. (b) Defensive stance, with arms crossed over head; note bent knee and step backwards.

3. At the same time, step back on your back leg and bend your knee toward the floor. This will lower the height of your head in conjunction with your block, and thus prevent your head from being hit with the stick or club.

Fighting: Defenses and Counterattacks

The way to respond to an attack is to prevent it from reaching you, as we've discussed above. The second step, then, is to counterattack with multiple blows, kicks, or gouges aimed at vulnerable areas. Sometimes you may have to attack first, as when a person threatens you and you believe an assault imminent.

Adjusting Your Distance

Whether you are attacking or defending, you need to adjust your distance according to whether you want to make contact with your blows or evade the assailant's blows. When you attack (or counterattack) you may have to move toward the assailant, since he may be out of range, or your attack may be aggressively pushing him back. To move forward, step with your front foot first, then your rear foot. Take small, quick, even steps. Keep your torso erect. If the assailant attacks you, move out of range. Step back with your back foot first, then your front foot. Sidestepping will be discussed in the section on weapons defense.

Attacking Vulnerable Target Areas

As was discussed under the eight rules of fighting, you should aim your attack primarily at five vulnerable areas: eyes, neck, nose, groin, and knee (refer back to Figure 3.1). You should attack one or more of these areas in rapid succession, in combination with other attacks, and keep attacking until you have incapacitated the assailant. Your target depends upon three things: (1) the area you can reach; (2) what is left exposed; and (3) your distance from the assailant. In this section, we will discuss specific ways of attacking vital points.

The Eyes. As the most vulnerable area of the body, eyes can be gouged, causing temporary or permanent blindness and excruciating pain. Don't be squeamish about attacking the eyes. The rapist's eyeballs won't fall out. And in a crisis situation, this technique may save your life.

THE THUMB GOUGE.   Grasp the sides of the attacker's head with both hands, fingers spread apart. Firmly hold his head with your fingers and forcefully thrust your thumbs into the eyes (Figure 3.11).

THE FINGER JAB.   Spread your fingers apart and keep your fingers and wrist rigid. Using full force, jab with all four fingers into the eyes (Figure 3.12). If the assailant is wearing glasses, aim just under the rim of the glasses and continue up into his eyes.

The Neck.   Various blows to the neck can cause excruciating pain, unconsciousness, and severe injury.

BLOW TO THE ADAM'S APPLE.   The Adam's apple is an easy target because in men it projects outward. Use a clenched-fist punch (Figure 3.13) or an elbow smash; clench your fist and bring your arm up to chest level. Using your other hand to hold your fist

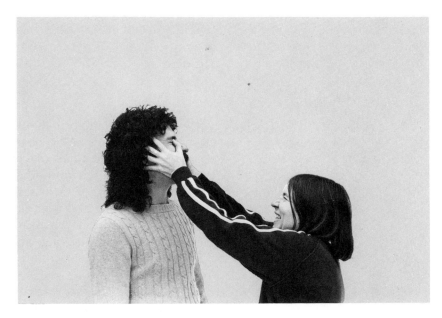

FIGURE 3.11.   The thumb gouge to the eyes.

FIGURE 3.12.   The finger jab to the eyes.

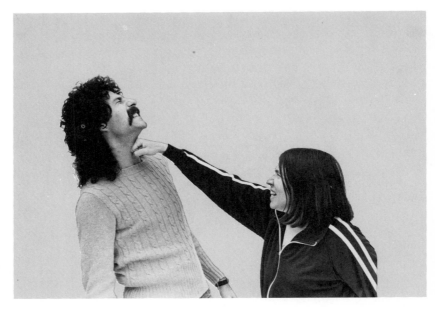

FIGURE 3.13.   The clenched-fist blow to the Adam's apple.

FIGURE 3.14.   Elbow smash to
the Adam's apple.

will strengthen the thrust of the attack. Keep your elbow bent and
thrust it into the assailant's Adam's apple (Figure 3.14.)

TWO-HANDED BLOW TO BACK OF NECK.   The back of the neck is
usually attacked as a secondary area in combination with another
attack. For example, after you have kneed the attacker in the groin,
he may double over, exposing the back of his neck. You can attack
this area with a two-handed blow, as shown in Figure 3.15. Clasp
one hand over the other, palms together and thumbs crossed.
Wind up and strike the rear of the neck with the side of your hand.

EXTENDED KNUCKLE BLOW TO WINDPIPE.   In order to get
maximum force into this relatively small hollow area, attack the
windpipe with an extended knuckle blow. The mechanics of punching are the same as in the clenched-fist punch. To extend your
knuckles, first make a clenched fist. Then keeping the first two
fingers together, extend their knuckles outward (Figure 3.16a).
Strike the windpipe with these two extended knuckles (Figure
3.16b). Keep your wrist tight.

The Nose.   The nose is a sensitive area that bleeds readily.
Blows to the nose are painful and can cause unconsciousness.

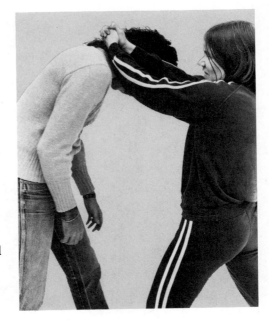

FIGURE 3.15. A two-handed blow to the back of the neck.

BLOW TO BASE OF NOSE. Strike the base of the nose with the heel of your hand, with your force directed back and upward (Figure 3.17). Flex your wrist back slightly and use the same force as if you were punching.

TWO-HANDED BLOW TO NOSE. Using the two-handed blow as described above in the attack to the back of the neck, smash the bridge of the assailant's nose (Figure 3.18).

The Groin. The groin is a highly vulnerable area in males. A forceful blow to the groin causes excruciating pain and unconsciousness and can thus immobilize the attacker. *Caution:* Because the assailant may *expect* a blow to the groin and be prepared for it, your attack to this area must be a complete surprise.

KNEE TO GROIN. This is a close-range attack. Lift your knee forcefully under the groin as if you were going to execute a snap kick (Figure 3.19).

GROIN PULL. Reach your hand between the assailant's legs, grab his testicles, squeeze, and pull (Figure 3.20).

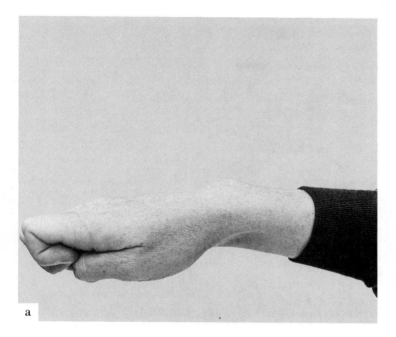

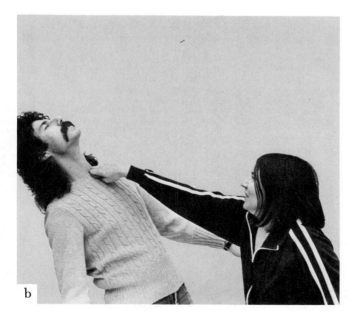

FIGURE 3.16.   Extended knuckle blow to windpipe. (a) Clenched fist
with knuckles of first two fingers extended. (b) Extended knuckles strike
windpipe.

FIGURE 3.17. Blow to base of nose with heel of hand.

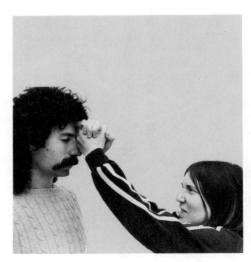

FIGURE 3.18. Two-handed blow to bridge of nose.

FIGURE 3.19.   Knee to the groin.

FIGURE 3.20.   Groin pull.

UPWARD BLOW.   If the assailant is wearing very tight pants and you are unable to grab his testicles, make a clenched fist (Figure 3.21a) and, using the bony area of the arm, forcefully strike upward between his legs into the groin (Figure 3.21b).

The Knee.   The knee is highly vulnerable, and even forty pounds of force directed at the knee cap will cause enough damage to immobilize the attacker.

SNAP KICK TO KNEE.   If the assailant is in front of you, execute a snap kick to his kneecap (Figure 3.22). If you are not already in your stance, assume your stance *as* you kick. Otherwise, you will telegraph your attack.

SIDE KICK TO KNEE.   If the assailant is at your side, execute a side kick to the knee (refer back to Figure 3.6).

BACK KICK TO THE KNEE.   If the assailant has grabbed you from behind kick his kneecap with a back kick (refer back to Figure 3.7).

FIGURE 3.21.   Example of an upward blow to the groin. (a) Two-handed clenched fist. (b) Forceful blow to the groin.

FIGURE 3.22.   Snap kick to knee.

Releases and Counterattacks

Your object is simply to get away safely. If an assailant is attacking you, you should try to prevent him from reaching you by blocking and/or moving out of the way or by breaking out of his hold if he has grabbed you. Then you should immediately counterattack in a vulnerable area, incapacitate him, and run away. Incidentally, if you are attacked from the rear, there may be no warning, and you should be prepared to assume your basic stance instantly and tuck in your chin. This will aid in giving you stability and power and in protecting your air supply.

Let us now discuss techniques you can use to break out of situations where you are being grabbed, held, or choked, and possible counterattacks.

When Grabbed by the Wrist.   The most vulnerable area on someone grabbing your wrist is the upper knuckle area of his thumb. In breaking out of a wrist grab, direct your force into this area. As in any defense, your response must be immediate. Get into your stance, yell, and forcefully break out of the grab. *Note:* If any wrist grab release doesn't work, immediately kick the attacker in the knee or use some other counterattack.

ONE-HANDED GRAB.   If possible, grab the fist of the arm being held (Figure 3.23a). If the assailant's thumb is on top, grab your own fist from the top; if his thumb is underneath, grab your fist underneath. Using the power coming from your legs as well as your arms, forcefully break into the direction of his upper thumb joint (Figures 3.23b and c). Counterattack with a kick to the kneecap if you are the proper distance away for kicking. If you are within punching distance, attack a vulnerable, accessible area such as the throat.

TWO-HANDED GRAB.   If an assailant grabs you with two hands, kick him in the kneecap. When he releases his grasp, run away.

When Grabbed by the Arm.   The same principles are used to break an arm grab as for a wrist grab; you break into the upper joint of the assailant's thumb. If he has come up from behind and

FIGURE   3.23.   One-handed wrist grab release. (a) Assailant grabs wrist. (b) Grabbing own fist. (c) Grip is forcefully broken.

a

grabbed your arm (Figure 3.24a), pivot toward him and break out of the grasp, using the same upward and outward motion you would use in an upward block (Figure 3.24b). Your counterattack options are the same as for the one-handed grab. If the attacker has grabbed both your arms from the rear, use the back kick to break out of the hold.

When Grabbed by the Hair. If you have long hair and the assailant grabs it, put your hand between his hand and your scalp. If you have short hair, put both your hands over the assailant's hands and press down. In both cases this will help alleviate the pain. Do not attempt to pull away from him. Rather, move toward him and attack with a kick to the knee, a punch in the throat, or a jab to the eyes.

Choking Attack. Breaking a choking hold is a relatively simple maneuver, and the same technique is used in attacks from the front or the rear. The principle to remember is forcefully to use your raised shoulders to break out of the hold.

b

c

FIGURE 3.24.   Arm grab release. (a) Assailant grabs arm from behind. (b) Breaking from grasp.

REAR CHOKE RELEASE.   If attacked from the rear (Figure 3.25a), immediately get into your basic stance. At the same time, follow these steps:

1. Raise your arms directly over your head, reaching for the ceiling.
2. While you are raising your arms, forcefully pivot 180 degrees so that you are facing the attacker. Keep your arms raised and your hands reaching for the ceiling until you have completely broken out of the hold (Figure 3.25b). Otherwise, the release will not work.
3. Counter attack by gouging the attacker's eyes with your thumbs (Figure 3.25c).
4. He will probably respond by trying to grab your wrists. As he does so, knee him in the groin (Figure 3.25d).
5. Finish the attack with a two-handed blow on the back of the neck (refer back to Figure 3.15).

FIGURE 3.25. Rear choke release. (a) Assailant attacks from behind. (b) Raising arms and pivoting, (c) hold broken. (d) Eye gouge counterattack (e) Knee to groin (next page).

e

FRONT CHOKE RELEASE. If attacked from the front (Figure 3.26a), immediately get into your stance. Simultaneously:

1. Raise your hands beyond his arms, directly over your head (Figure 3.26b).
2. Forcefully pivot about 120 degrees so that you have broken out of the hold but can still see the attacker (Figure 3.26c). (*Never* turn your back on the assailant.)
3. Counterattack with one of the following: an elbow to the throat, a thumb gouge to the eyes, a punch to the Adam's apple, or, if you are out of range, a side kick to his knee (see earlier figures).

Escaping a Bear Hug. A bear hug occurs when an assailant grabs you from the front and pins your arms below the elbow (Figure 3.27). There are several responses which you can make. You can knee him to the groin, execute a groin pull, or use an upward blow to the groin. In the case of a rear bear hug (Figure 3.28a) you can use the groin pull or give an upward blow to the groin. An-

a

FIGURE 3.26. Front choke release. (a) Assailant attacks from the front. (b) Raising arms over head and (c) pivoting forcefully breaks the attack. (d) Possible counterattack—elbow to throat.

b

c

FIGURE 3.27.   Front bear hug.

other option is to crouch down as low as possible in your stance and thrust your buttocks back into the assailant as hard as possible (Figure 3.28b). This will cause him to lean forward, giving you some space to move. Immediately pivot to your side, slam your elbow into his stomach (Figure 3.28c), and execute a rear kick to the knee (refer back to Figure 3.7).

REAR ATTACK: FOREARM AROUND THE THROAT. In this instance, the assailant grabs you from behind, both arms around your shoulders or one arm around your shoulders and the other over your mouth (Figure 3.29a). He may try to pull you backward. One option is to use the groin pull. Here is another:

1. Start by getting down in your stance and create a space between you and the attacker by swinging your hips in the direction away from the assailant's arm holding your shoulder (Figure 3.29b).
2. Put your arm that is closer to his armpit through the space you have created, reach up, and forcefully yank his hair back

a

FIGURE 3.28. (a) Rear bear
hug. (b) Buttocks thrust hard into assailant. (c) Elbow blow to the
stomach.

b

c

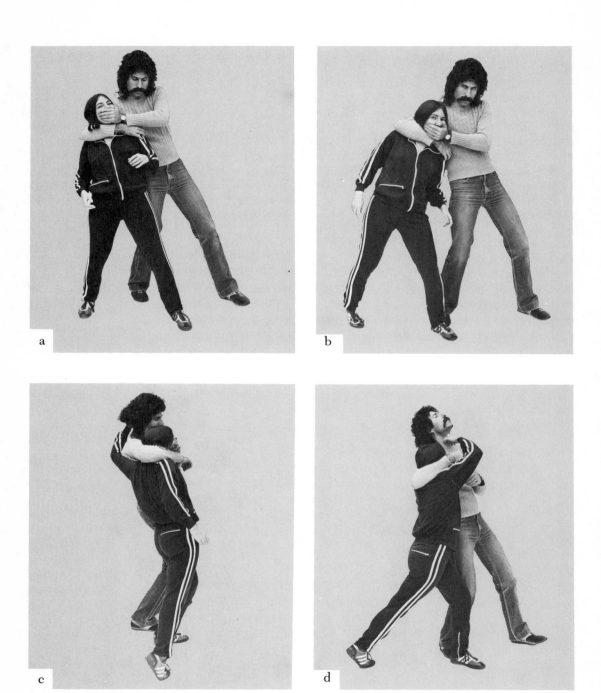

FIGURE 3.29.   Forearm around throat release. (a) Assailant grabs from behind, keeping one hand over mouth. (b) Swing hips away to create space. (c) Grab hair and yank head back. (d) Pivot and punch Adam's apple.

from the roots. This will jerk his head back and expose his Adam's apple (Figure 3.29c).

3. Pivot toward him, and punch him in the Adam's apple with your free fist (Figure 3.29d).

PINKY RELEASE.   This release technique is for when an assailant grabs you from the rear, with his arms around your shoulders. Or when you are on your back and he on top of you, or when you're sitting and he comes up from behind and is strangling you. "Pinky release" means go for his little fingers. The pinky release may not incapacitate the assailant, but it will free you to make a counterattack. To do this:

1. Turn your palms facing away from you.
2. Position the thumbs against the base and to the side of the assailant's pinkies.
3. With your thumbs positioned, wrap your fingers around his pinkies. Simultaneously press your thumbs into the sides of the pinkies and pull the pinkies to the side and back sharply (Figure 3.30).

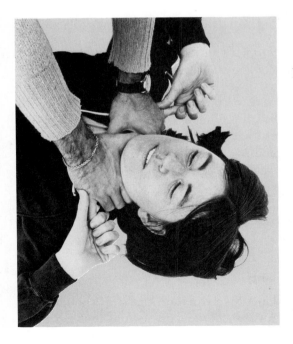

FIGURE 3.30.   The pinky release.

REAR GARROTE ATTACK. You must *instantly* react to this extremely dangerous attack because it will be only moments before your air is cut off. The most important consideration is to protect your air supply.

1. The second you feel a thong strangling you, pivot forcefully toward the assailant, keeping your arms down at your side. The pressure will then be on the bony part of your neck rather than on the soft tissue.
2. Immediately gouge the assailant's eyes, knee him in the groin, and smash down on the back of the neck. Do this viciously and forcefully.

Defense Against Attacks When You Are Down

If you are lying down (if knocked to the ground or awakened in bed, say), you are obviously not in as good a position to fight back as if you had taken your stance. Nevertheless, you still can incapacitate the assailant.

1. If he has pinned you down on your stomach, try to roll over onto your back.
2. If that isn't possible, try to free an arm and punch him in the Adam's apple.
3. If the assailant is on top of you, depending upon your respective positions, you could execute a groin pull, jab your fingers into his eyes (Figure 3.31), smash the base of his nose with the heel of your hand, or punch him in the throat. Any of these counterattacks can be made even if he is choking you, because your defense will force him to stop his attack.
4. If he has thrown you down and is not yet on top of you, brace yourself with your back arm and kick him in the knee or the groin (Figure 3.32).

The key to your defense is flexibility. Analyze the situation for vulnerable areas to attack.

Escaping Multiple Assailants

This is an extremely dangerous situation that you should make every effort to prevent. An aerosol weapon such as tear gas is ex-

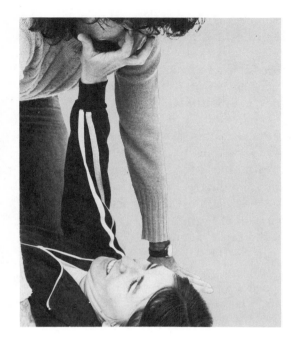

FIGURE 3.31. Jabbing fingers
into assailant's eyes from lying position.

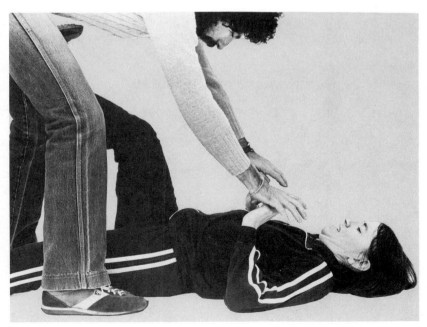

FIGURE 3.32. Kicking assailant in groin from lying position.

tremely effective against more than one person; this is discussed later in this chapter. Don't hesitate to shoot the attackers in the eyes and then run.

If there are two or more attackers, usually one will grab you in order that the other(s) may have free rein to attack you (Figure 3.33a). What must be done is as follows:

1. Determine which attacker is the most dangerous to you and deal with this person first. Usually, it is someone other than the person who is restraining you.
2. Use the attacker who is holding you for support and leverage, and kick the person who is coming in to attack you. Aim your attack at the knee or groin (Figure 3.33b). Then deal with the other assailant(s) in the same manner.
3. The last one to consider is the person holding you. Break out of his grasp in the way you would handle an attack from the rear and then incapacitate him (Figure 3.33c). Of course, if you were being injured by him, you would act to incapacitate him first.

FIGURE 3.33.   Release from multiple assailants. (a) One person often acts to restrain to allow others to attack. (b) Use attacker doing restraining for leverage and kick other(s). (c) Incapacitate attacker doing restraining.

Dealing with an armed assailant was covered in Chapter 2. Sometimes you have a choice as to whether or not you will fight back. When someone is attacking you with a knife, however, you must fight back. Try to use something as a block or shield. You may be able to wrap a coat around your arm, snap a jacket (as you would snap a towel) at the knife, or use a purse or briefcase as a shield. You may be able to use an umbrella or stick as a weapon, to counter the attack. Incidentally, if you are being attacked with a stick or bat, the force of the blow is greatest at the end of the weapon. Therefore, sidestep the attack and/or move in close and execute a kick, blow, or gouge.

Caution: The skills covered in this section are more advanced than the skills described in the preceding sections. If you wish to use them, they require repeated practice, until you become proficient in their use. If you attempt to use them without mastering their use, you may be ineffective.

The descriptions that follow of defenses against knife attacks are given for a right-handed attack. The left-handed attack will require using the opposite arm and moving to the opposite side from that described.

Overhand Knife Attacks. First ascertain the direction of the attack, whether it is coming to the outside or down across your body.

ATTACK TO THE OUTSIDE
1. First use an upward block with your left arm (Figure 3.34a). Make contact with the assailant's arm between his wrist and his elbow. Make sure to complete your block by bringing his knife arm beyond your body line.
2. At the same time you block, straighten your right leg, pushing down and back (as if you had punched).
3. Make a V form—fingers together and thumb extending out to the side—with your right hand. Grab the assailant's knife arm from below with the V, keeping your wrist stiff and with your arm at the same angle as your rear leg (Figure 3.34b). What you are doing is using your whole body as a brace against his downward thrust. Remember to keep his knife arm beyond your body line.

4. Let go of his arm with your left arm (the arm your originally used to block) and bring your left hand underneath and around the attacker's knife arm and grab the fleshy part of his thumb. (Your thumb is now on the back of his palm and your fingers are curled around his thumb.) Maneuver your right hand so that you bring your right thumb up next to your left thumb. Both of your thumbs are pressed down in the middle of the back of the attacker's knife hand (Figure 3.34c).

5. Now twist his wrist outward and downward so that his wrist and elbow are at right angles (Figure 3.34d). To visualize how to twist the wrist, imagine that, if the assailant's hand broke off, it would fall palm down on the ground. Apply maximum power and continue to do so until the assailant drops the knife. Kick it out of reach. Continue your attack until you have incapacitated the assailant. (If at any point you are unable to complete the defense, kick the assailant in the knee.)

ATTACK ANGLED DIAGONALLY ACROSS BODY.   Your response to this attack is similar to that for the outside attack, with a few differences.

1. Since the attack is aimed toward your right side, block with your right arm. (If you block with the left arm, you would go against the assailant's direction of force and, in addition, would bring the point of the knife across your body.) Make sure your block brings the knife arm beyond your body line.

2. Then, with your left hand, immediately grab the fleshy part of the assailant's thumb in the same manner as for the outside attack. Your left thumb is on the back of his knife hand.

3. Place both of your thumbs side by side and apply pressure so as to bring the knife toward the left, away from you but across the assailant's body. Continue to twist at right angles until he drops the knife.

Underhand Thrusting Attack.   Ascertain the direction of the attack, whether it is coming toward your left, right, or middle.

ATTACK TO MIDDLE OR RIGHT SIDE

1. As the knife is thrust at you (Figure 3.35a), grab the top of the wrist of the assailant's knife hand with your right hand.

2. *At the same time*, pivot away from the attack (Figure 3.35b). by picking up your right foot and placing it about twelve

a

b

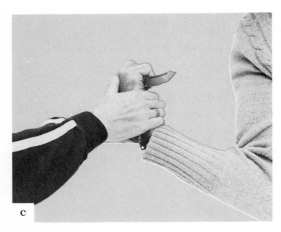

c

d

FIGURE 3.34. Defense against overhand knife attack to outside. (a) Upward block to knife arm. (b) Grab knife arm with other arm. (c) Press both thumbs on back of knife hand. (d) Twist wrist outward and downward. (e) Assailant drops knife.

e

inches behind your left foot. (Make sure that you are in your stance.) This move will prevent you from being hit by the knife because you literally move your abdomen out of the way.

3. Using the assailant's momentum, pull him forward (Figure 3.35c) and put him in a reverse arm lock to break his elbow and force him to drop the knife (Figure 3.35d). Execute the reverse arm lock as follows:

   a. As you pull him forward, wrap your fingers around the fleshy part of his thumb and twist his wrist outward.

   b. Pass your left arm over his arm, close to his armpit and your armpit, and bringing your right elbow close to your left elbow, grasp your left arm above the elbow.

   c. Apply leverage against his elbow joint (which only moves one way) by forcefully lifting up with your right arm and snapping down with your left. The joint is forced against its normal range of motion. Make sure you have a stable base of support and execute this movement quickly and forcefully so as to snap the elbow. Complete the defense by thrusting your left elbow into the assailant's throat (Figure 3.35e).

FIGURE 3.35.　Defense against underhand thrusting knife attack to middle or right side. (a) Assailant thrusts knife. (b) Grabbing wrist and pivoting away. (c) Pulling assailant forward; beginning reverse armlock. (d) Breaking assailant's elbow. (e) Counterattack: elbow thrust to throat.

e

THRUSTING ATTACK TOWARD LEFT SIDE.   If the knife is thrust at your left side, it is more difficult to pivot to the left as in the thrusting attack described above. Therefore, as the knife is thrust at your left side, do the following:

1. Sidestep to the right with your right foot first, then your left.
2. At the same time, grab the top of the wrist of the knife hand with your left hand.
3. Turn your right hand so that the palm is toward the assailant and your fingers are pointing down. Take your right thumb and place it in the middle of the back of the assailant's hand, and grab the assailant's hand with your fingers of your right hand.
4. Release your left hand and place your left thumb next to the right thumb (as in the overhand knife defense), grabbing his hand with the fingers of your left hand.
5. Twist upward and inward so that the knife is pointed away from you, to force the assailant to drop the knife.
6. Counterattack with a kick to the knee or other appropriate attack.

Use of Legal Hand Weapons

It is best not to have to depend on any weapon other than your own body. A hand weapon may not be accessible when you need it, or, if available and not used properly, it could be taken away from you. It is important, however, to be aware of what you can use as a weapon if you choose. Develop your own fighting skills first, and use other weapons as backup, if you desire. Choose weapons that you like, that you commonly carry with you, and practice with them until you are highly skilled. When you employ a hand weapon, follow the same principles you would use in fighting.

Guns

Local laws differ in respect to guns. Never employ a gun as a weapon unless you fully understand how to use it and have practiced so that you are proficient. If you wish to consider using a gun as a weapon, check with your local police department or the National Rifle Association concerning gun use and safety. I would recommend against the choice of a gun as a weapon if there are any children in the household or if anyone in your household has a bad temper or a history of depression or mental illness.

Tear Gas

Tear gas is an aerosol weapon that can rapidly and effectively incapacitate an assailant. When a person is sprayed in the face with the chemical, he or she experiences pain, a stinging and burning sensation, temporary blindness (at least several minutes), and difficulty in breathing. The individual may also experience a period of disorientation, with a feeling of panic, dizziness, and a loss of balance (see Figure 3.36).

The two types of tear gas in common use are CN gas and CS gas. When sprayed in the face, CN reacts within two to three seconds. For CS to have an immediate reaction, the person must be hit in the open eye otherwise the reaction may be delayed for approximately twenty seconds. Some individuals are not affected by CN tear gas, including persons under the influence of alcohol, certain drugs, those with certain mental illnesses and those experiencing hysteria. This is because CN acts on the nerve centers that control pain, and a person with a condition that has depressed these pain centers will not be affected by the gas. CS gas, however, is a much

FIGURE 3.36. CS tear gas. (Courtesy Personal Protection Systems and W.C.A.)

more powerful chemical and will be effective on almost everyone.

Local laws differ as to the legality of tear gas use. In California, unlawful use or illegal possession is a felony, and in order to legally use tear gas for self-defense, you must take a certification course. It is also a felony in the United States to carry tear gas aboard a commercial aircraft. Check with your local law enforcement agency concerning the law in your state.

I recommend carrying tear gas as a deterrent and as a back-up weapon in self-defense. I prefer CS tear gas, and carry a canister with me when I go out.

Aerosol weapons have a range of approximately ten feet. If you carry tear gas with you, make sure that it is readily accessible, not in your purse or back pack. It is best to carry it in your hand or put it on your key ring, on a belt, or in an easily reachable pocket.

Umbrella

Place one hand halfway up the umbrella (furled or open), the other on the handle. Jab the assailant's throat with an upward thrust.

Rolled-up Magazine

Ram the edge of the magazine into the throat with an upward thrust.

Hardbound Book

Hold the closed book with both hands. Jab a corner of the book upward under the nose or into the throat. You could also slam the flat surface of the book into the assailant's face.

Keys

Support one key with your thumb and first finger. Put a second key between the second and third fingers. Your hand must be turned so that the thumb is on top and the pinky is on the bottom. Make sure the keys are firmly supported. Jab the keys into the assailant's eyes or windpipe.

Purse

Do not swing your purse at an attacker, because he will easily be able to block your attack. Hold the purse with both hands and ram it into the assailant's throat or push it under his nose. You can carry items in your purse that convert into weapons—such as a teasing comb. Thrust the comb at the assailant's eyes or at his windpipe.

Hat pin

Carry a hat pin where it can be easily reached, as in the lapel of your coat. Hold the pin securely in your hand and employ a quick jabbing motion. Jab the pin at vulnerable exposed skin areas.

High Heels

Stomp the assailant's instep with your heel. Since this will not incapacitate him, you must follow with an incapacitating attack. Another tactic is to take off your shoe and, holding it firmly, jab it into the windpipe or the eyes.

Pen

Hold the pen firmly between your thumb and fingers and thrust it into the assailant's windpipe or jab it into his eyes.

You can find many other weapons to use; be innovative. Remember: Take your stance, use force and power, and be prepared to continue your attack with an incapacitating kick or blow. Do not wind up. The assailant could easily grab your weapon. Avoid giving any hints that could announce your attack.

Home Practice

Home practice is essential for proficiency. And proficiency in your skills is essential for an effective defense.

Whether you practice with a male or a female is a matter of personal preference. The attitude of your practice partner, however, must be supportive of your efforts. If you practice with a female friend who doesn't take you seriously or who discounts your intent to learn, or if you practice with a male friend whose ego gets in the way, you are preparing yourself to lose. Students have told me that in practicing with their boyfriends they were unsuccessful in thwarting attacks. If the failures continue, students would begin to doubt the effectiveness of techniques learned in class. In one such case I asked the student if she were really angry at her friend during practice and if she were willing to incapacitate him during the session? The student replied, "Of course not!"

I explain to my classes that sometimes the only way to break out of a hold is to force the attacker to let go by incapacitating him. In real situations, their anger and outrage will add higher levels of adrenaline to the blood, giving them additional strength and endurance. Both anger and outrage were absent from the home practice sessions described above.

It is important in setting up a practice session to have some rules to practice by. Practice only with a supportive partner. Make an agreement that the partner will release his or her hold or stop the attack if you simulate a counterattack that is incapacitating. The partner should agree not to release his or her hold too easily, or you will develop a false sense of what will and will not work. Aggressive body language (the "Don't mess with me!" signal) on the part of both the resister and the attacker should be incorporated into home practice sessions as early as possible.

Key Points to Remember

- Fight to win. When you make the decision to fight back, do so with the full commitment to win.
- In most cases, immediately and forcefully resist an attack or threatened attack.

- Yelling is a potent weapon that should be utilized throughout your defense.
- Attack vulnerable areas, strike through the target, your objective being to incapacitate the assailant immediately. The target areas include eyes, base of nose, neck, groin, and knee (see Figure 3.1).
- Anger is your most powerful weapon. Get angry. Use your voice and body language to communicate your anger and outrage.
- Think in terms of flexibility according to individual situations. Analyze the situation in terms of vulnerable areas available for you to attack, and how you can attack them.
- Fight according to the correct mechanical principles of force, balance, speed, and distance. Stay in your stance.
- Maintain eye contact with the assailant in order to intimidate him and to avoid telegraphing your defense.
- Learn and practice your fighting skills until they become second nature.

Chapter 4

Prevention:
Your Best Defense

Why is prevention so important? For one thing, it's easier: *It's far easier to prevent a dangerous situation from occurring than to fight your way out of one that has occurred.* This applies whether you're in the home or out, on foot or in a car, alone or with others, as will be discussed in this chapter. I firmly believe that most crimes against people and property can be prevented. It is principally a matter of planning ahead, staying alert, and using common sense. These points can be illustrated in preventive measures you can take.

Before You Leave

Before you go out, even if you're leaving for only a short time, make sure all doors and windows, including the garage door, are not only closed but locked. Carry keys with you. It is unwise to try to hide a key somewhere outside the house, since a potential intruder may see you retrieving it. Better to leave a spare key with a neighbor whom you trust.

Wear sensible clothing that will not hamper movement.

Street Safety

Know exactly where you are going and plan how to get there. If the address is unfamiliar, get complete directions and make sure you understand them. Be aware of possible troublesome areas, and try to avoid them. Learn the locations of police and fire stations, all-night gas stations and stores, even telephone booths.

While on the Street

Be aware of your surroundings and environment. When you pass alleys or other places where someone could hide, look directly at them. Watch for anything suspicious or unusual. If you sense something wrong, act on your feelings and take action to avoid the situation. As we discussed in Chapters 2 and 3, use body language that expresses confidence and self-respect. Walk as if you mean business: pace brisk, shoulders back, eyes looking forward, your expression confident, alert, and aware.

Nighttime is especially dangerous, of course, because vision is limited (yours and the fact that the assailant is less likely to be observed), and because fewer people are on the streets. Walk in well-lighted places; avoid deserted streets, and do not take shortcuts through dark alleys and parks. Walk on the side of the street facing oncoming traffic; this will permit you to see a suspicious car, rather than let it come up from behind you. If there are few cars, you might consider walking in the middle of the street (in the direction of oncoming traffic).

Tear Gas.   A canister of tear gas (if legal in your state) or similar product in an accessible pocket or in your hand is especially useful at night or in dangerous areas. (See section on tear gas in Chapter 3.) Although it is vital to be able to rely on your own body in case of attack, tear gas is a good defensive weapon that is very useful in case of threatened attack. It is also excellent in warding off multiple attackers.

Hitchhiking.   Hitchhiking or accepting rides from strangers increases the risk of being assaulted. A popular bumper sticker reads: "Nobody rides for free. . .gas, grass, or ass." If someone calls you over to a car to ask for directions or assistance, walk on by or, if appropriate, call out, "Sorry, I can't help you." If a car approaches you, turn around and walk in the opposite direction.

Packages and Purse Snatching. Try not to load yourself down with packages or books. If you find yourself having to fight or flee, drop whatever you are carrying that might hinder your action. Also, don't carry large sums of money or anything valuable that you can't afford to lose. While it is best not to carry a purse since this can make you a more likely target, if you do carry one, avoid wrapping the strap around your shoulder, neck, or wrist so you won't be injured if the purse is grabbed. Carry your purse close to your body or under your coat; a dangling purse is an invitation to easy snatching (see Figure 4.1). Credit cards, driver's license, and other identification should be concealed.

If you are confronted by an armed mugger, cooperate with him if all he wants is your valuables. Things, of course, can usually be replaced; you cannot. The mugger wants two things, the valuables and an escape; he is not usually interested in hurting his victim.[1] After you have handed over what the mugger wants, if he then threatens force, you may decide it is appropriate to fight back. (Ways for dealing with an armed assailant were discussed in Chapter 2.) You are now fighting to protect yourself, not property.

FIGURE 4.1. A dangling purse is an invitation to purse snatchers.

If Followed.   If you think you are being followed, turn around and check. Don't be concerned about looking silly. To verify your suspicion, change your pace or cross the street. Use car windows or store windows as mirrors to see behind you. If you determine that someone is tailing you, assess the situation and choose your options. Look for a safe place—an inhabited or lighted area, an open store, restaurant, or gas station. If nothing like that is seen, an alternative is an enclosed telephone booth. Once inside the booth, lean against the door to keep it from being opened and call the police. (If your local service does not provide free emergency calls, always carry coins for a local call with you—preferably concealed in your clothing.)

If you decide to run, do it suddenly and make as much noise as possible. Yell "Fire!" as you run, rather than "Help!" Yelling "Fire!" may be helpful in bringing immediate assistance, whereas yelling "Help!" may bring no assistance at all.[2] If at all possible, run to where there are people rather than to an isolated area. If you are being chased and run to an occupied house, consider smashing a window (use a shoe, rock, or any heavy object). Banging on the door for help takes time and may not bring any assistance. Often, people do not want to become involved. Although smashing a window is not legal, you may be saving your life. Breaking the glass will attract the immediate attention of the occupants (who most likely will call the police) and may act as a deterrent to the person chasing you. If you cannot find an occupied building, consider breaking a store window to set off a burglar alarm. This, too, may act as a deterrent. If you decide you must fight, use methods described in Chapter 3.

If Approached.   When a stranger asks you a question, answer briefly and walk away. Keep your distance. Your body language indicates that you are either vulnerable or unassailable, and it is best to be cool and aloof toward strangers. If the stranger persists in talking to you, don't feel obligated to continue the conversation. If he won't leave you alone, yell as loudly as you can to attract others' attention, and be prepared to use other self-defense techniques, if necessary.

Harassment.   How you deal with street harassment depends on what you perceive the harasser's possible motive to be. A person

But only if you're prepared to pay for it.

trying to bother you in public needs you for an audience. He wants
you to respond to him—by expressing embarrassment or perhaps
even by finding his attention flattering. He may, on the other
hand, be testing you to see if you are a potentially vulnerable rape
victim. Your approach to a harasser should be based on his physical
distance from you and your perception of his intent or actions. If
you are walking down the street and someone calls out, "Hey baby,
want some action?", your reaction might be embarrassment or
anger; however, a good response usually is no response. Watch the
harasser with your peripheral vision, but don't let on that he exists
at all. If you walk with confidence and self-assurance, a deadpan
expression on your face, it accomplishes two things: first, you won't
let yourself become angry by responding to this type of annoyance;
second, the harasser does not receive the satisfaction of having
bothered you. The "no response" pattern is useful as long as the
harasser does not follow you or persist in his behavior.

If you find yourself in the extremely upsetting situation of being
pinched or fondled in public, it's best to respond with loud outrage, such as "Keep your hands to yourself!" since the fondler
counts on your embarrassed silence. If you do remain silent, you
can count on being upset for many hours afterwards.

If you are confronted by an exhibitionist or "flasher," put on a
deadpan expression, say nothing, and walk away toward an area
where there are other people. Incidentally, exhibitionists are not
necessarily harmless, and I suggest you report the incident to the
police.

On Returning Home

Make sure no one is following you. Particularly after dark, do not
linger at your front door. Have your key ready and enter immediately.

Few things are as terrifying as awakening in the middle of the
night to find a stranger standing over your bed. Your home should
be your refuge, but without precautions it can also be a dangerous,
isolated area if you are confronted by an intruder.

The San Francisco Police Department estimates that 85 to 92
percent of break-ins are of the *opportunity* type. That is, through
carelessness or ignorance, a resident readily gives a criminal the

Safety at Home

opportunity to enter his or her home. *Most intruders can be kept out* through a combination of physical security and personal safety practices. Let us consider physical security first.

Physical Security

A secure house is a deterrent. You cannot live in a fortress and probably do not want to, but you can make forced entry into your home difficult enough to discourage the average criminal. First let us consider the entries that can be forced—doors and windows.

Protecting the Portals. Before we can consider door locks, peepholes, and the like, we have to consider the door itself. It's foolish to spend money on strong locks if all an intruder has to do is kick the door in or pry it off its frame.

Hollow-core doors can be kicked through in seconds. It's best to replace them with sturdy wooden doors (in high-crime areas, a metal door), or else reinforce them with steel plate on the inside, which will prevent attempts to cut around the lock. Doors with glass panels can be reinforced with quarter-inch plexiglass.

Oftentimes the door frame itself needs to be reinforced. A warped door with a gap between it and its frame, or between the rough door frame and the finish frame, can be penetrated by an intruder with a pry bar. If such is the case, remove the finish frame and reinforce the rough frame with pieces of plywood secured to the rough frame with two-inch-long screws.

Hinges also need to be looked at. If the door swings outward, the hinge pins will be exposed, and all the intruder has to do is remove the pins and lift the door out of its frame. If you find exterior doors or doors leading to the outside to be constructed in this fashion, you can do the preventive maneuver shown in Figure 4.2, which will allow the door to remain closed even if someone removes the pins from the hinges.

Every door that leads to the outside should be equipped with a deadbolt lock. Locks built into the door knob, such as those shown in Figure 4.3, are flimsy and easy to pick; they can also simply be ripped out of the knob or opened with a credit card slipped between the door and frame. If your lock is insecure, install an auxiliary deadbolt lock, such as that shown in Figure 4.4, with a one-inch bolt and hardened cylinder guard above your other lock. Use two-inch screws to secure the strike plate to the rough frame.

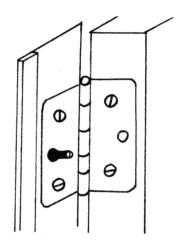

FIGURE 4.2. How to secure a door with outside hinges: Remove two middle screws from each leaf of the hinge. In one hole insert a strong screw or concrete nail and allow it to protrude half an inch, as shown. Drill out the other hole at least a half inch so the protruding screw opposite will be easily recessed in the hole when the door is closed.

FIGURE 4.3. Example of an insecure lock. (Courtesy Schlage Lock Company.)

FIGURE 4.4. Auxiliary deadbolt lock. (Courtesy Schlage Lock Company.)

Many kinds of locks are available in a wide price range, from complex devices to locks offering reasonable security.

A deadbolt rim lock (Figure 4.5) is installed on the inside of the door. The bolt can be either a one-inch deadbolt or the interlocking jimmy-proof variety. Again, securely attach the strike plate to the rough frame. If glass is within forty inches of the lock or if the door is paneled, a double cylinder lock should be installed (Figure 4.6). (Important: a key should be left close to the inside keyhole—but further than an arm's reach away from the door—to assure fast exit in case of fire.)

A special note about chains: Easily broken through in seconds, they are virtually useless as security devices. Indeed, they are dangerous because they give the illusion of security.

If you have a solid door, it's good security to install an extra-wide angle viewer (with a 180-degree range). The peephole will permit you to look out but will prevent the person outside from looking in.

With sliding glass doors, your objective is to keep the door from sliding or being lifted up and out of its track. A length of dowel or a broomstick in the track offers little protection. One way to secure a sliding glass door is to drill a downward-sloping hole on the inside channel into the top portion of the door frame (Figure 4.7) and insert a 5/16-inch pin or eyebolt. Another way to secure a sliding door is to install a slide bolt (Figure 4.8), on which a padlock may be used for extra security when you are not at home.

Special consideration is needed for the door that leads to the house from an attached garage. Doors between garage and home are often flimsy and provided with inadequate locks. Be certain the door is reinforced and secured with a deadbolt lock.

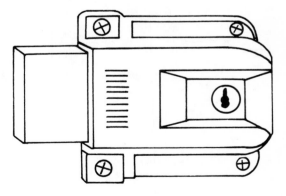

FIGURE 4.5. Deadbolt rim lock. (Courtesy San Francisco Police Department.)

FIGURE 4.6. Double cylinder lock. (Courtesy Schlage Lock Company.)

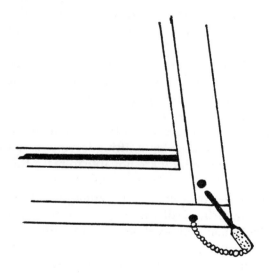

FIGURE 4.7. Sliding glass door protection.

Back and side doors are not readily noticeable from the street, and so intruders often choose one of them as the break-in point. Therefore, pay special attention to reinforcing back and side doors and locking them with secure deadbolt locks.

FIGURE 4.8.   Slide bolt for securing sliding glass door. (Courtesy San Francisco Police Department.)

Window Security.   Glass windows are obviously extremely vulnerable. A burglar could smash a window if he dared make the noise; and he could chisel away the putty if he dared take the time. (*Note*: If your window putty is very old and dried out, a burglar could just lift the window out.) Windows at ground level are, of course, more accessible than those at higher levels, but determined intruders can use ladders, fire escapes, and trees to enter homes. Usually, the burglar will not risk smashing a window, but will look for a quiet and quick entry—easily accomplished by prying open a window with a bar or screwdriver.

With double hung windows, a small crowbar placed between the sill and the lower window sash can develop a lifting force of a half ton. Locks commonly found on the market are not able to resist this type of force. What you can do, however, is drill a hole through the inside sash where it overlaps the top window three quarters of the way through the top window sash. Drill the hole at a downward angle and insert a 5/16-inch-diameter eyebolt. Do this on both sides of the window (see Figure 4.9).

Windows can be *locked* in ventilating positions. This can be accomplished by screwing a quarter-inch screweye into the side tracks so that the window can be opened enough for ventilation but not enough to admit an intruder.

Casement windows are more difficult to break through than double hung windows. They are usually opened with a removable metal crank from the inside. For security, remove the crank when not in use and place it in a nearby drawer.

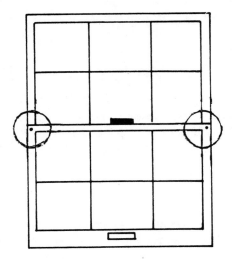

FIGURE 4.9. Securing a double hung window.

Sliding glass windows, like sliding glass doors, should be secured from sliding or being lifted out of their tracks. Secure them as you would sliding glass doors.

Louver windows are poor security risks; these should be either replaced with another type of window or protected with an iron grate or grille.

Windows at street level and those facing a fire escape require additional protection, provided by grilles or grates. If the window faces a fire escape, you can purchase ornamental bars that open from the inside. Or, in addition to the existing window, you can install quarter-inch plexiglass sheets (except windows facing fire escapes). Remember to secure your basement windows; since basements are usually not occupied, burglars often choose them as entry points.

The Garage. Often overlooked as a target for intruders, garages usually are full of things that a burglar can turn into cash, such as power tools, bicycles, motorcycles, and camping equipment. Since the garage is usually isolated from the rest of the house, the intruder can take what he wants with little chance of being seen.

In order to remove temptation from the burglar, I suggest that you either have light-colored shades or whitewash the inside of garage windows. If you can afford it, protect garage windows with case-hardened steel grates or iron bars. Otherwise, secure the windows as suggested above in the discussion on windows.

A single lock on the garage door is inadequate to keep a burglar from prying it up on the opposite side and crawling into the garage. This lock requires reinforcement. Several methods may be used: (1) Add another bolt and padlock to the side opposite the lock; (2) add a top center hasp (made of hardened steel and installed with carriage bolts through the door); or (3) install a pair of cane bolts to the inside of the door.

Other Deterrents

Once you have gone about securing the possible entrances to your house or apartment, you can turn your attention to other measures which will act as deterrents to would-be intruders. Let us consider a few of these.

Lighting. Proper illumination, both inside and outside your home, acts as a good deterrent against unwelcome entry. Lighting outside your house should cover front, side, and rear entrances, as well as any other point at which an intruder could gain entrance or hide. A good location for exterior lighting, in addition to the porch, is the eaves of the house. Outside lights should be left burning all night; a timer or photoelectric cell will automatically turn the lights on at dusk and off at dawn. Lights should be bright enough so that you can read your watch and be able to spot the silhouette of an intruder.

Interior lighting will suggest that someone is inside; absence of interior lighting in the evening is a sure sign of an empty house. Timers should be installed on lights in various areas to give your home a lived-in look. Living rooms and bathrooms are good areas to light. A light in the bathroom at various times of the evening and night especially gives the home a lived-in appearance.

Shrubbery. Shrubbery should never block the view of your front door. Nor should shrubs or trees be in or next to your path from the garage to the house. They make ideal hiding places from which to enter your home or to assault you when you are leaving or returning. Any shrub that might give an intruder the cover of darkness should be lighted at night.

Alarm Systems. These provide a second line of defense against someone breaking into your home. Good physical security measures will deter easy entrance, lights will expose the criminal, and a good loud alarm will announce his presence. The psychological element of a loud unexpected sound may be enough to send him fleeing.

Two types of alarm systems are available. The perimeter alarm usually relies on magnetic switches mounted on doors or windows. When the door or window is opened, the alarm sounds. Area alarms consist of detectors within the house. Devices include pressure pads, ultrasonic units, photoelectric sensors, and infrared detectors. The alarm sounds when an intruder enters the area protected by the device.

Alarms vary widely in type, quality, and features. Some can be installed by the buyer and some require professional installation. First determine your needs, then shop around until your requirements and your budget are satisfied.

Marking Your Valuables. Property engraved with an identifying number is less likely to be stolen. Marked property is more difficult to sell because thieves can be more easily prosecuted if they are discovered with the stolen property in their possession and because identifying marks permit the police to return stolen property to their rightful owners. Police commonly suggest that you inscribe your driver's license number or social security number on valuable property in and around your home. An engraving tool can often be borrowed from police departments that participate in an "Operation I.D." program. Usually the police will, upon return of the tool, provide the user with a decal (see Figure 4.10) placed in windows and elsewhere around the house. Decals warn the potential intruders that items of value have been marked for ready identification by law enforcement agencies.

Dogs as Deterrents. Dogs provide a ready alarm system. They are territorial in nature and will warn you if anyone is on your property or trying to enter your home. An intruder cannot know,

FIGURE 4.10. Example of Operation I.D. decal. When placed in one's front window or door, this decal sets would-be burglars on notice that valuables have been inscribed with the owner's driver's license number to make the items harder to fence and easier to recover. (Courtesy San Francisco Police Department.)

from the sound of a barking dog or from its looks, whether or not it is attack-trained. A medium-size to large dog is probably best for both appearance and bark. If your house is entirely surrounded by a fence, a dog left outside can be a first line of alarm and protection. Otherwise, since the dog can't do anything to protect you if it is locked up in the backyard, I suggest leaving it inside when you are not at home, at night, and when a stranger is visiting.

Personal Safety Precautions

You may have the best locks and security devices in the world, but all are completely worthless if, through carelessness or poor personal safety habits, you allow an intruder to walk in through the front door. Keep your doors and accessible windows locked when you are at home as well as when you are away. Windows can be opened for ventilation, but keep them *locked* in ventilating position so that an intruder can't pry the window open and crawl through. I know of a woman who left her patio door open when she was taking a shower. When she finished and walked into her bedroom, she found a strange man inside. She had the presence of mind to yell at the top of her lungs, "Get out of here!" and the man fled. She was lucky.

In this section, I'll give some suggestions on ways to reduce your risks to personal safety.

Telephone Precautions. Telephones either can be a wonderful aid in personal security or, through unwise use, can place you in danger.

LISTING. List your last name and the initials of your first and middle names (*Smith, J. B.*) in the telephone directory, but give no address. It is unwise to list your first name, because criminals and disturbed persons sometimes look through telephone books for women's names. You can also opt to have an unlisted number or use a fictitious name in the directory if you do not wish to be listed in the telephone book. Street address directories, available in some areas, list street address, name, and telephone number. If you wish your name and address *not* to appear, inform the telephone company business office.

TAKING CALLS. Be cautious about what you say on the phone. Although a stranger may, of course, phone for a legitimate purpose, he may also phone to find out if you live alone or if you are at home, to harass you, or for some other criminal purpose. Never give any personal information on the phone. If the caller asks for the man of the house, never let him know that he is out, that you are alone, or that there is no man of the house. You can say that he is unable to come to the phone and offer to have the call returned. The same procedure applies when you are unsure about the legitimacy of any call: Tell the caller that it is inconvenient for you to speak just then and offer to return the call. In this case, check the telephone directory for the name and number, if one is actually given.

If you receive either obscene or harassing phone calls, it is best to hang up immediately. If the calls persist, continue the procedure of hanging up and file a report with the police. Then notify the telephone company. Obscene and harassing phone calls are prohibited by federal and state laws. You may request to have your number changed at no charge, but before the telephone company will do this, you may have to keep a log of the obscene or harassing calls for a week or two. If you are being threatened, the telephone company might decide to tap your line in order to catch the criminal.

TELEPHONE ANSWERING DEVICES.   Answering machines can be a signal to a criminal caller that you are not at home and/or can give out personal information about you. To minimize this risk, your message should give as little information as possible about you or your whereabouts. Instead of leaving the message that you are not at home, I suggest a message such as, "I am unable to come to the phone right now."

The Front Door.   It is unwise to place your name on the front door or mailbox. From it, a potential intruder might easily check your name in the telephone directory and call to find out if anyone is at home. If you feel that your name must be on the mailbox, I suggest using your last name only.

No law in America states that you must answer your door or let someone in—including the police and the FBI. Be very wary. Being alone with a stranger in your home is being in an extremely isolated, vulnerable position. The police can enter against your wishes only if they have a warrant or if they have reason to believe that a crime is in progress. But you have the right to see the warrant and demand identification.

Be assertive. Only let the person at the door in the house if you really wish to do so. When you answer the door, identify your caller to your satisfaction before permitting him or her entry. First check through the peephole to see who it is. (If it is nighttime the porch light should be left on so that you are able to see who is out there.) If you decide to answer the door, ask through the door who the person is and request proof of identification. Remember, chains are no barrier between you and the person at the door, so don't rely on one to protect you.

If the caller states that he is from a company (such as the electric company) verify the identification by checking the number of the caller's company in the phone book, and by calling the company to check that the visit is legitimate. Do not rely on a phone number the caller gives you. It could be a trick. By letting the person know that you are calling to check on the number, he is put on notice that someone else knows that he is there.

If you have a dog, keep it on a leash with you. If you lock the dog in a room or put it outside, it cannot help protect you. If the caller is at your door at an inconvenient time for you (you may be alone, for example), tell him that you will reschedule the visit at a more convenient time. Then, make the appointment for a time when you are not alone. Above all, *don't feel that you have to let the person into your home.* Your sense of well-being and your safety is more important than his time.

Emergency Plans. The best way to handle an emergency is to plan in advance what you will do should a crisis situation arise. The following are some suggestions as to measures you can begin to put into effect now in hopes that you'll never have to use them.

SAFE ROOM. It is a good idea to designate one room of your house as a safe room. Usually your bedroom, it is where to go to should an intruder break into your home. Since interior doors are very flimsy, the door to this room will have to be reinforced. Install a deadbolt lock, and, if the door swings outward, pin the hinges. Make sure that the windows to this room are secure, but that you have an escape exit. If you are on the second floor or above, have a rope or chain ladder available for quick exit.

This safe room should have a telephone with emergency numbers taped to it. An extension phone is less satisfactory for this purpose because an intruder can take another phone off the hook and thereby prevent you from completing the call. If you cannot afford a second phone, install a jack in the room in which you have your phone as well as in your safe room. Simply take the phone into the safe room at night when you go to bed, or be prepared to run with it into the safe room if you need to. Another alternative is to keep a C.B. radio in your safe room, which wouldn't be affected if your phone lines were cut.

SECRET CODE WORDS. Consider establishing a special secret code word or sentence with members of your family or trusted friends. You could use this word or sentence to warn someone of danger or to let them know that you are in danger and to get help immediately. If an intruder is in your home and you have come face to face with him, you may be able to convince him that someone is expecting your phone call. You could then make a phone call and leave your secret message. Such a code message could be: "*Call the pharmacist* to fill my prescription." Translation: "Call the police."

CONFRONTING AN INTRUDER. If you hear someone breaking

into your home, leave if doing so is safe. Before you do, go to your safe room and call the police for help. If you come home and find that someone has broken in, don't go in. You don't want to surprise a burglar or block his escape route; he may become violent. Go to a neighbor's house or the nearest phone and call the police.

What if you come face to face with an intruder in your home? The answer is, what is more important, you or your property? I would suggest that you try to stay cool, ask the burglar what he wants, and cooperate with him only as long as your bodily safety is not being threatened. If you consider that he is threatening you with bodily injury or rape, fight back, if feasible, to incapacitate him, and then get out of the house and call the police.

TELEPHONING FOR HELP. The police will give immediate priority to a call reporting a crime in progress or bodily injury. When you call the police in an emergency situation, make sure to let them know that it *is* an emergency and tell them clearly what is happening. If an intruder is in your house or you hear someone trying to break in, make sure that the police understand that the crime is *in progress*. Give them the location, your phone number, your name (if you wish), and any description of the individual or weapons he may have. Try to stay as cool as possible.

Good Neighbors. Good neighbors can help one another in many ways to prevent crime. A neighbor can watch your home while you are away for the day or a longer time. A neighbor can keep your spare key for you. This is much wiser than placing it under the welcome mat or in the mailbox.

Neighborhood groups or block clubs can significantly reduce the incidence of crime on the block. They are often organized with the assistance of the local police department, which provides technical advice on crime prevention. Neighbors meet about once a month. They cooperate to report suspicious activities, to keep an eye on homes when the residents are away, and to learn personal and property safeguards. Members of the group put warning decals on their doors and windows, notifying potential intruders that their premises are being watched.

Some neighborhood groups, especially in inner cities, have developed a whistle system. Neighbors carry whistles on their keychains, to blow when in trouble, when hearing someone else blowing his or her whistle, or when they find someone acting suspiciously.

When You Are Away. Your main objective is to prevent a burglar from learning that you are not at home. Instead of stopping deliveries, I suggest that you ask a neighbor with whom you have developed a "good-neighbor policy" to pick up newspapers and other material left at your door. If you notify the newspaper, the garbage collection service, and other regular services that you are going to be away, who is to say that you are not notifying an employee who is part of a burglary ring? You can ask your neighbor to put trash in your can and to put out your trash. Leave your key with the neighbor so that your mail can be collected and the position of your shades or drapes moved periodically. If someone is loitering around your house, the neighbor can call the police to investigate.

Tell as few people as possible that you will be away and do not talk about it in public. Use timers on your lights and radio. Do not disconnect your phone. This is a sure sign of a prolonged trip. Have your grass mowed or your snow shoveled, depending on location and season. If you have a dog, you may be able to arrange to have a friend (or the good neighbor) walk and feed it. The animal will be more confortable in its own surroundings and your house will be safer. Before you leave, make sure that you have locked all doors and secured all windows.

For Apartment Dwellers

Apartment buildings can be equipped with special security equipment and services or they can be a risk to the personal safety of the residents. When you rent an apartment, look for a building with a security guard or a doorman twenty-four hours a day who requires proper identification of all visitors. If there is no doorman or guard, the apartment building should at least have an electrically controlled door-opening system and an intercom so that each tenant can identify callers before permitting them to enter. Hall lighting must be adequate and be maintained. Light bulbs should be either protected or located so that an intruder cannot turn them off. Fire stairs should have doors that open in only one direction. Try to rent an apartment above ground level since a ground-level apartment is especially vulnerable and requires additional window security.

Regarding keys: The landlord or superintendent probably has a master key, which is required in case of fire or other emergency.

You have no evidence that whoever has the master key is reputable or responsible; he may lose the key, or it may be stolen from his apartment. If the key that opens your door is in the hands of a burglar, your whole security system is very much in danger. Sloane, in *The Complete Book of Locks, Keys, Burglar and Smoke Alarms*, recommends the following:

I urge you to remove the cylinder, take it to your locksmith and have him change the combination. Then if the janitor argues about it, ask him why he tried to enter your apartment. It's better to argue about this minor lease violation than it is to lose your valuables or even your life because some building employee turned crooked or was careless about his master key.[3]

Make sure that your door has a peephole and a deadbolt lock and is made of solid wood or is reinforced. Make sure also that the window leading to the fire escape has extra protection. Accordian-type grates or ornamental iron grilles that open from the inside will prevent entry from the outside but will permit you to exit in case of an emergency.

Tenants in apartment buildings should get to know one another. Acquaintanceship promotes building security. In addition, tenants' groups can collectively put pressure on uncooperative or negligent landlords or superintendents to provide and maintain adequate building security.

While Driving or Riding

An automobile can enhance your personal safety; it relieves you of having to use relatively unsafe inner-city mass transportation systems at night, for example. On the other hand, a car has its dangers, for, if a potential assailant gets control of it, you can be trapped in an isolated area. By using common sense and being alert, you can prevent this from occurring.

The following are some suggestions for car safety:

- Maintain your car in good working order, with safe tires and an adequate amount of gasoline.

- Always thoroughly check your car before getting in. Make sure no one is hiding inside.

- While doing stop-and-go driving, keep your car doors locked and windows high enough so no one can put an arm in.

- *Never* pick up hitchhikers.

- Park in attended lots, if possible. If you have to leave a key with the attendant, leave only the ignition key. Whenever you can, lock your car.

- Avoid parking in deserted places. At night, park in well-lighted areas.

- Do not leave anything of value on the car seat. Put it in the trunk before you reach your final destination.

- When buying gasoline, it's best to give the attendant only the key to your gas tank, not your full set of keys. (A wax impression could be made of your house or car keys.)

- Always have your key ready when going to your car. Be alert (see Figure 4.11).

FIGURE 4.11. Be alert when going to unlock your car. (Note position of tear gas canister.)

- If you have a flat tire in an area you feel might not be safe, try to keep driving until you reach a safer location.

- In the event of car trouble, lift the hood and attach a white handkerchief to the antenna or left door handle as a signal for help. Then get back in the car and lock the doors. Keep the windows closed except for ventilation. At night leave your emergency flashers on. If someone stops, lower your window a crack and ask the person to call for assistance. Do not let a stranger get into your car or give you a ride to a garage.

- If you pass someone who is stranded or who needs assistance, don't stop, but drive to the nearest phone and call the police.

- If a suspicious-looking car is following you, drive to the nearest police or fire station, or to the closest place where people will be.

- If you are in danger of being harmed while in your car, start blowing your horn until assistance arrives.

- If someone is in your car threatening you or forcing you to drive to an undetermined location, try to bring attention to yourself—either to attract help or to scare off the assailant. If you know you will drive past a police or fire station or hospital, quickly turn in and start sounding your horn. A drastic alternative is to cause a minor accident. (I am suggesting this because your life may very well be in danger if you permit the assailant to take you off to an isolated area.) At a stop light or stop sign, gently (so it won't cause injury) hit the car in front of you; the driver will undoubtedly jump out and come over to your car.

- When returning home, have keys in hand in order to unlock your garage and house doors quickly.

While waiting for a bus, streetcar, or other public transportation, stand near others who are also waiting. If the area is dark or deserted, stand near an occupied building or in a lighted area.

Once on the bus or streetcar, be aware of those around you. Sit in the front half of the coach, in the seat closer to the aisle, so that someone can't trap you in the window seat. If someone begins to bother you, get up and notify the driver immediately. If you sense other trouble on the bus, get off as soon as you can, as it is always best to avoid possible trouble.

When you arrive at your stop, be aware of those who alight with you. If you feel that you are being followed, follow the suggestions given earlier on street safety, pages 83 to 87. When it is dark, always try to get off in lighted areas and use only well-lighted streets to reach your destination.

Recreation Precautions

In order to keep your leisure activities enjoyable, I suggest that you consider certain commonsense precautions to keep you safe and free from undue worry or stress.

Jogging and Hiking

Jogging and hiking pose serious problems because, by the very nature of these sports, women can often find themselves alone in isolated areas; we are all familiar with gruesome newspaper articles describing women being attacked along solitary trails. One need not stop hiking or running, however; there are several precautions you can take to reduce the risks to your safety.

First of all, I strongly recommend you not jog nor hike alone. Although this may be an inconvenience, you're much better off with a companion. You should also avoid going out on completely untrafficked trails. It is usually unwise to jog at night, especially since the areas in which you are apt to be running are usually emptier of people at night. I also suggest varying your routes and times, so a potential assailant won't detect your daily pattern and try to stake you out.

If you have a dog, take it with you and don't tell anyone that your dog wouldn't hurt a fly. (Actually, if you're being threatened, you may be surprised at how unfriendly your dog can become.) Avoid being friendly to people you meet; be cool and aloof. Let your body language demonstrate that you are aware, alert, and possess self-confidence. You may wish to consider arming yourself with a canister of tear gas when you go out (see Figure 4.12a and b). It can be a powerful weapon to thwart a would-be assailant.

For a Safe Social Life

The key to personal safety is to keep out of isolated situations with people you don't know well enough to trust. As I said earlier, rape will never occur between two people who respect each other

FIGURE 4.12.   Using tear gas as defense while jogging.

as equal human beings. Let's consider, then, steps you can take for a safe social life.

A lot of socializing in America goes on in bars, and some men frequent bars with the express purpose of picking up sexual partners. If you are friendly with a stranger in a bar or permit him to buy you a drink, his interest in you will probably increase, and you may have difficulty shaking him off. You should be especially aware of strangers who offer to escort you home. In addition, be alert for men lurking outside of a bar; often they prey on women who have had too much to drink and so are more vulnerable. Whether you're in a bar, out on a date, or at a party, don't allow yourself to be manipulated into being alone with someone you don't know or trust. As I've said, most rapes occur in the victim's home or in the rapist's home.

It's best to meet a date you don't know well in a public place. It's also wise to carry money for a phone call or taxi, should the need arise; you want to avoid having to depend on your escort to take you home. (If it becomes necessary to take a taxi alone and you don't have money with you, take the cab anyhow, and ask the driver to wait outside your home while you go inside for the fare.)

Women need to learn to be less polite and hesitant and more assertive and direct in their behavior and language. This is especially true on dates. Thus, I suggest avoiding behavior toward your date that implies anything other than how you feel. If, for example, you are at a party and your date wants you to go into a bedroom with him but you don't want to, make it clear through your body language and verbal language so that he understands this—otherwise you will find yourself in an unwanted situation.

Your self-respect and assertion of your rights as a human being are supremely important. If you think a man will not ask you out again because you won't "perform," tell yourself he's simply not worth going out with. Everyone, both male and female, is under peer group pressure to conform to certain expectations. It's important to resist these pressures and establish clear and honest communication with the person you are dating.

Many of the personal safety precautions discussed earlier in this chapter apply equally to children as to adults, but some special precautions are applicable to children. Young children need special

Protecting Your Children

protection. When they are old enough to understand, they must be taught to take precautions for their own personal safety and the safety of other members of the household.

Sitters

Hiring babysitters should not be casually done. A girl sitter may appear to be nice, but for all you know she may have a boyfriend with a drug habit. It's best to use sitters recommended by friends as competent and reliable. A prospective sitter should be interviewed with one or both of his or her parents present. Do not permit the sitter to invite friends over during babysitting. Make sure that the sitter is familiar with your family's safety rules and emergency procedures (how to call the police or fire department) and leave a number where he or she can reach you. It's best also to lock up valuables and important papers rather than leaving them out where they are tempting.

Home Safety

Children should be instructed in family emergency plans and given frequent safety drills. They should be shown how to phone police and other emergency numbers. They should be taught never to open the door to a stranger or give information about the family to anyone who comes to the door or calls on the phone. If someone phones, for example, and asks to speak to a parent when the parent is not at home, the child should respond by saying, "My mother (or father) is unable to come to the phone. May I have him (or her) return your call?"

Practice with your child a secret code word, as discussed earlier in this chapter.

Children and Strangers

Children should be taught to keep away from strangers and, in particular, they must learn that no one has the right to touch them in intimate places. They must be encouraged to report to you, without fear of punishment or ridicule, if they have been approached, robbed, hurt, or molested by anyone. They must be instructed to refuse rides or even to go close to a car from which a stranger calls to them. And they must learn to refuse all gifts from strangers. They should be taught not to play alone in alleys, deserted areas, or public restrooms. If a child has a paper route, is selling cookies door to door, or the like, it should be arranged that a friend go along. When collecting payment, the child should not go into a strange person's home.

Senior citizens are especially vulnerable to attack because their physical or mental capacities may be diminished. Many older women in poorer circumstances live alone in run-down, high-crime areas. They are often dependent upon public transportation. In addition to the personal safety suggestions offered throughout this chapter, there are some special cautions that older persons should consider.

For the Senior Citizen

Safeguarding Pension Checks

Purse-snatchers and muggers are often aware of the time of month when senior citizens receive social security checks; hence, special precautions need to be taken. The best way is to arrange to have the check deposited directly into one's bank account. When going to the bank, a senior should also arrange to go with a companion, and to vary both the route and the day and time. Money received from the teller should be immediately and discreetly put away, and on leaving the bank, one should remain aware and alert, especially to the possibility of someone following. It is best to pay bills with checks or money orders, and to pay them by mail.

Purse Snatching

In addition to the precautions described above in this chapter, a few added suggestions can be made for the senior citizen. If possible, do not carry a purse. If you do carry one and someone is trying to grab it, rather than be wrestled to the ground and be hurt, let it go or turn it upside down and let the contents fall out (so the robber will grab the wallet). If you fear that someone might try to grab your purse, consider dropping it in the nearest mailbox. Carry only a small amount of cash inside your purse, in addition, and, if there is a need to carry more, conceal it elsewhere on your person.

On the Streets

Tear gas (described in Chapter 3) is an excellent deterrent as well as a weapon which can be used by those lacking the same physical capabilities as a younger person. A shriek alarm, made from compressed air, sends off a piercing scream. Hold the alarm in an accessible pocket and use it if you are in danger—it is a good deterrent.

Because you look like such a vulnerable target, if possible, walk and take mass transportation with a companion, and vary your routes. Be especially cautious of strangers who offer assistance or ask for directions.

Security and Psychological Well-Being

The practices described in this chapter are designed to give you very detailed information concerning preventive measures. It is not my intention that you barricade yourself in your home. You can feel safer knowing that your personal safety practices and physical security measures act as a deterrent to assault. And the knowledge that you are prepared to act in case of emergency will go a long way in helping you achieve a sense of psychological well-being.

Chapter 5

Especially for
the Working Woman

As more and more women enter and reenter the work force, along with increased financial rewards come increased risks. "Job security" comes to mean not just secure tenure in employment but actual physical safety while at work. Women who travel on business become potential targets. Women who work irregular hours and those who must meet clients away from the office face the possibility of assaults. All working women are vulnerable to sexual harassment. What can be done about such threats?

People working in offices after a while begin to think of the work place as secure territory, though in fact it may not be. Rapport with office colleagues does not guarantee one against theft of personal possessions or freedom from assault, whether from outside intruders or even from fellow workers. Clearly, the best defenses, as in other activities I mentioned previously, are common sense and alertness. Let's see how this translates into specific steps for safeguarding your valuables and protecting your person.

The best place to keep your purse is in your desk drawer—locked. It (or anything else of value to you) should never be left out

**Safety in the
Office**

in plain view. The same is true of valuables in your coat pockets. You should protect keys, pieces of identification, checkbooks, and credit cards with the same degree of care that you do cash. Even if everyone in your office is honest, some visitors to the building may not be.

Physical assault in offices can occur in a number of places, such as restrooms, elevators, and isolated areas.

Restrooms can be located in infrequently trafficked areas, and assaults can and do take place there. If such is the case with the women's restroom in your building, ask another woman in the office to walk with you. Be alert, and, if you sense something wrong, leave immediately.

Elevators also deserve scrutiny. Look inside the elevator before you enter; if an occupant looks suspicious, take the next car. When you get on an elevator, stand near the control panel; that way, if you have trouble, you can press *all* the buttons so that the elevator will stop at every floor. If a suspicious-looking person gets on, leave before the door closes. Before leaving the elevator, carefully observe the corridor.

Special precautions should be taken to avoid isolated locations in office or public buildings. If you must walk through dimly lighted hallways in infrequently traveled areas, be as cautious as if you were walking the streets at night.

A potentially dangerous situation arises when you work after hours, on holidays, or weekends, especially if you are by yourself in the office or building. Make sure that you are familiar with your building's security system. Learn how to summon help quickly. Let someone know where you are and when you are expected home. It's a good idea to have a canister of tear gas or similar product with you and have it easily accessible. Trust your intuition and act on it: If your supervisor asks you to work late or on the weekend, and you don't feel comfortable doing so, either decline it or take a friend. Also, if feasible, find out who else is working overtime; perhaps you can coordinate hours and exchange office phone numbers in case of emergency.

Fighting Sexual Harassment

Sexual harassment, says Betty Harragan in *Games Mother Never Taught You*, is "women's most dangerous occupational hazard."[1] It can be defined as unsolicited and unreturned sexual advances, demands, or degrading sexual comments or remarks made to or about women. It can vary from off-color jokes or remarks to staring or leering, to pinching, patting, or touching, to subtle suggestions to see the man socially after work, to direct sexual demands. The woman most vulnerable to such harassment is the one most dependent economically on her job. The man most likely to make such sexual demands is someone with economic power over her, that is, her supervisor, although he could also be a co-worker.

Sexual harassment is widespread[2] and commonly condoned in the workplace. The message to women is *put up or get out*. Should a woman complain or refuse to give sexual favors, she can receive unfavorable performance evaluations, be denied advancement, be forced to quit, or be fired, and the man will most likely deny any wrongdoing and go unpunished. Company policy toward sexual harassment has often been to deny that it exists or to blame the woman. Unemployment applications filed on the basis of sexual harassment are often denied. And when the victim applies for a new job, she often gets a bad recommendation. The picture in the workplace has been extremely bleak.

How to Fight Sexual Harassment

Although the situation is difficult, women do not have to be helpless victims. And because some women have been courageous enough to fight back, conditions are slowly starting to change and companies are slowly beginning to set policies to eliminate sexual harassment and thus protect themselves against lawsuits.

In April 1980 the Equal Employment Opportunity Commission issued regulations that explicitly forbade the sexual harassment of employees by their supervisors in government (federal, state, or local) or in private business employing fifteen or more persons. Under these new regulations, employers are charged with preventing and eliminating sexual harassment, whether physical or verbal. In enforcing these regulations, the EEOC is empowered to ask awards for back pay and reinstatement of employees fired for reasons based on improper sexual motivation.[3]

An interesting analysis of the politics involved in socializing with work colleagues and the disadvantages to the women employee can be found in Chapter 14 of *Games Mother Never Taught You*.[4] Harragan states that any time a woman becomes involved in sexual activities with an employee of the same company she loses status in the company and forgoes any real chance for advancement.

Although in the male-dominated game of sexual harassment the odds are stacked against the female, there are steps that women can take to ward off unwelcomed sexual advances. The approach, of course, depends upon the seriousness of a particular incident and the options open. Let us consider different steps you can take.

Assertiveness Techniques. This method, used at a first approach, has the aim of trying to defuse harassing behavior. Ignoring unwanted advances will not make them go away. Flirtatious behavior that indicates you are interested (when in reality you are not) encourages unwanted advances. Assertive behavior implies the communication of your feelings in a way that is not challenging to the other's ego. At this stage, it would be unwise to challenge or embarrass the individual in front of other people. Remember, your aim here is to defuse the behavior, not to escalate it. If the harasser is embarrassed in front of his peers or subordinates, he will lose face and never forget it.

Ask to speak to the person privately (but not in an isolated area). Suppose, for example, your supervisor pinches you. Instead of accusing him ("Take your hands off me; you should know better!") or saying nothing, which will encourage repeated attacks, say something like, "I feel uncomfortable when you pinch me." Here you are utilizing *I* to communicate your feelings instead of *you*, which is accusatory. If the use of assertiveness techniques does not ward off the sexual harassment, subsequent steps should be taken.

So what?

Document Your Case. Keep a journal documenting the episodes of harassment. List names, dates, times, and witnesses, and describe the incidents. Also document any physical or emotional side effects you may have suffered as a result of the incidents. If you felt that psychiatric counseling was necessary, be sure to include this in your documentation. Carefully preserve your records. In short, realize that you are gathering evidence, which is a prime requisite to help you prove your case—in court, at an administrative hearing, to personnel officers, or in order to collect unemployment benefits.

Go Through Channels. Through your company's formal apparatus (with copies of memos or forms for your files), complain to your company grievance committee, your union, or the personnel department. You may not get satisfaction, but you are gathering and providing documentary evidence. If you are forced to go to court, and you have exhausted all official channels (and have this documented in writing), the company cannot use the excuse that you did not give them a chance to correct the situation.

Talk to Other Women in the Office. If other women in your office have had similar problems, find out if they would be willing to corroborate your charges. If you can find an ally, suggest to her that she also keep documentary evidence. You may also consider discussing this problem with a woman in a higher managerial position and trying to enlist her support.

Write to the Chief Executive Officer. This letter to the Chief Executive Officer should be sent to no one else in the company (but keep a copy, of course, in your file). Document the sexual harassment in terms of time and money lost to the corporation as a result of the activities of the employees specified in the memo.[5]

If You Lose Your Job. If you quit or are let go, write a detailed letter to the personnel department detailing your case and the lack of satisfactory corporate response.

Unemployment Insurance. If you file for unemployment insurance, consider that the company may well contest your claim. Be prepared to document your case. If you consider it helpful, seek legal advice.

Going Public. The media may be useful in exposing sexual harassment to the public, giving unfavorable publicity companies would rather avoid. Publicly owned corporations are accountable to their stockholders, and governmental agencies are accountable to the public.

Legal Remedies. In October 1979, the U.S. Supreme Court refused to hear an appeal by Western Electric Company of a suit won by Cleo Kyriazi and joined by more than 2,000 other women in a class action suit. U.S. District Court Judge Herbert Stern had ruled in October 1978 that, among other things, Kyriazi was "underrated, underpaid and denied promotional opportunities because of her sex; that she was harassed by her male co-workers and that she was [fired] on account of her sex and in retaliation for having lodged a complaint of sex discrimination."[6]

In March 1980, a superior court judge in Alameda County, California, awarded two women $275,000 in a sexual harassment suit. Karen Seritis and Teri DeLoach claimed that their former union leader, Ray Lane, and Local 28 of the Hotel and Restaurant Employees and Bartenders International Union denied them job opportunities after they turned down Lane's sexual offers.

Judge Robert H. Kroninger found that over the years, Lane had persistently pursued a course of conduct with women seeking employment, soliciting them to engage in sexual acts with him or third persons, offering them employment as prostitutes and pornography entertainers and boasting that his position with the union and his underworld contacts made it prudent to comply with his requests. It was also established that the union had long known of Lane's conduct.[7]

If you believe that you have been subjected to sexual harassment at work, you can file a complaint with the Equal Opportunity Commission. The EEOC will notify your employer of the complaint and investigate the charges. Although it is illegal for an employer to retaliate against an employee for filing a charge, you should realize that you run the real risk of being fired.

If you are fired because of sexual harassment, in order to sue under Title VII of the 1974 Civil Rights Act for back pay and reinstatement, you must file a complaint with the EEOC. You have 180 days to file (more time in some states). For your case to have a chance for success, it is advisable to have documentary evidence of the type described above. For more information about procedures, contact your regional EEOC office and your state equal employment agency.

The following groups may be able to offer advice on suing and filing charges of sexual harassment:

- Boston—Boston Alliance Against Sexual Coercion, (617) 482-0329

- Chicago—Women Employed, (312) 782-3902

- New York City—Working Women's United Institute, (212) 838-4420

- San Francisco—Women Organized for Employment, (415) 777-1781

- Washington, D.C.—Women's Legal Defense Fund, (202) 887-0364

An increasing number of women are traveling on business for their companies. The strange cities and unfamiliar surroundings required by jobs place them in potentially dangerous situations. By practicing prevention techniques, however, they can effectively reduce the risks to their personal safety.

For Women Who Travel

Trip Planning

Earlier, in the discussion on personal and property safety, I emphasized the importance of knowing your routes, locations of police and fire stations, and places where you could go for assistance. The same preparation applies when you travel. As a stranger, you are not as comfortable and sure of yourself as someone who lives in the area. If you are lost or look lost, your body language will indicate this. Since assailants choose vulnerable-looking persons as victims, your risk of being assaulted increases. Consequently, in planning your trip, you should get as much information as possible ahead of time about the places you will be visiting. A street map of any city you plan to visit will help. Become familiar with it. Locate the hotel or motel where you will be staying, the places you will be visiting, the locations of police stations. You may also speak to a travel agent or people who have been to the area. Travel books can also be useful.

Plan the wardrobe for your trip to include clothing appropriate to your business goals. Clothing, like body language, should not communicate double messages. Clothing can be attractive and still not impart the message that you are a sex object. I suggest that clothing be seasonable and stylish for the area in which you will be traveling. You want to blend as much as possible with the local population. If you stand out as a stranger, your risks increase. Shoes need to be appropriate to your outfit but at the same time must be comfortable and sturdy and must not restrict movement. Comfortable clothing and shoes are essential because, if you are uncomfortable, your level of awareness decreases and your vulnerability increases.

Leave an itinerary with dates and telephone numbers with a trusted person in your office and/or a friend or relative. Arrange to check back with that person at periodic intervals.

Travel Documents/Emergency Information

Carry with you the name of your health insurance company and policy number. Take the name and number of someone to contact in case of emergency. Safeguard any tickets or important documents and carry them with you rather than leave them in luggage or unattended.

Make a list of credit card numbers and the telephone numbers to call in case they are lost or stolen. Carry traveler's checks rather than cash. Keep a separate list of the numbers of these checks and the address and/or phone number to contact to receive replacement checks. Carry only credit cards essential for your trip. Make sure you understand the limits of your liability in case they are stolen, and consider getting extra insurance to cover this potential loss.

Hotel and Motel Security

Security of personal property is always a problem at hotels, primarily because the manager has a master key to your room and others in the employ of the hotel have access. Moreover, former guests and former employees may have made duplicates of the room key. And hotel door locks are notoriously easy to defeat.

Your hotel/motel security plan has three objectives—to safeguard yourself and your valuables and to prevent intruders from entering your room. Don't leave your valuables in your room when you go out. Hotels usually have a safe in which guests may leave things. To keep unwanted people out of your room when you are in, you can use a travel lock (a Yale Travelok, for example). It can be wedged in place between the door and the door frame and will keep the door from being opened from the outside. Be sure to lock your door whenever you leave the room—even only to go down the hall to the ice machine.

When you register, use your last name and first two initials, since a first name usually identifies your sex. Avoid unnecessary conversations with strangers and don't give out personal information. If a stranger persists in bothering you, summon the hotel management. If this isn't possible, you may have to use anger and aggressive body and verbal language (the "Don't mess with me" signal) in order to get the stranger to leave you alone.

Business Meetings

Be cautious about meeting a business acquaintance in an isolated area (such as your hotel room). If you can, you choose the place—corporate office or public restaurant. If you meet alone privately with a stranger, respectable businessman or not, you are running a risk. Be aware of this and plan your meeting places accordingly.

On the Road

When taking a taxi, don't assume the driver is 100 percent reputable. Make sure not to give him any personal information. If you let him know you are a stranger, alone, and unfamiliar with the area, you may be in for trouble. Have an idea of your route, and get an estimate of the fare in advance. If the driver makes unsolicited sexual advances, make a complaint to the police. (Taxi companies in most cities are licensed by the police, and many times drivers are disciplined if complaints about them are received.) Ask the driver for a receipt for the fare. You will then have his name and the name of the company. If you don't get a receipt, note the time, location, and name of the cab company.

Take as little luggage as possible on your trip. If you have a hold-over at the airport, use coin-operated lockers. (Don't ask some "friendly looking" person to watch your bags.) Guard your tickets and purse. If you require help with your bags, summon a skycap. Try to avoid checking your luggage; instead use carry-on bags. You will have less with you and be able to manage it by yourself. You also preclude the possibility of the luggage being lost, opened, or stolen before you claim it.

Special Precautions for Nurses, Flight Attendants and Social Workers

Women working in helping or service-oriented career fields need to take special precautions to prevent potential assault.

Nurses

Nurses as a group are more vulnerable to assault than the average female. Several reasons for this can be found. First, nurses often work odd hours and have to leave the hospital in the middle of the night or in the early morning, when few people are on the streets. Second, women in helping professions, women who have learned to serve others, are especially vulnerable to sexual assault. In Selkin's research on rape victims, for instance, one-fourth of the women in his Denver study who were attacked by strangers were responding to the assailant's request for help.[8] Third, nurses of necessity deal with the danger of potentially assaultive behavior from patients.

If you are a nurse, I suggest carefully reading and putting into practice the personal safety and self-protection concepts described in preceding chapters. Emphasize the psychological as well as the physical methods of prevention and self-protection. In addition, special techniques may be considered to control and prevent assaultive behavior in patients.

To avoid being attacked by a patient, try the following:[9]

- Try to recognize a potentially assaultive situation. Is someone angry? Does someone seem agitated? Does the patient have a history of violent behavior? Do you sense that something is about to happen?

- Try to defuse the situation before it gets out of hand. Even if you are tired, cranky, and extremely busy, treat the patient courteously. Ask him or her if there is a problem and offer to do something to solve it.

- Keep distance between you and the potentially assaultive patient. Don't see him or her alone. Be alert to possible attempts to back you into or lock you in a room. Don't get too close physically. Keep the door of the room open. Show professionalism and self-confidence, not fear, in your body language.

- Alert others to the possibility of assaultive behavior in the patient. You can signal a co-worker, for example, who can in turn call the hospital security guards or team that handles assaultive patients.

- Don't attempt to restrain the patient physically by yourself.

- If necessary, use tranquilizing medications to calm the patient. Drugs may be employed where permitted.

- If you have reason to believe that the patient has a weapon, don't attend him or her. Call the police to confiscate the weapon. You don't have to put yourself in needless danger.

If you are attacked by a patient, your reaction will depend upon the situation. If you can safely do so, break away and go for help. If you are trapped, incapacitate the patient; your job as nurse does not require you to let a patient endanger your life. If you can handle the situation safely by summoning help, breaking away, and/or blocking until help arrives, so much the better. But remember that you have the fundamental moral and legal right to self-defense if your life is endangered.

Flight Attendants

The nature of their work puts flight attendants in a high-risk category. They must travel to strange cities and stay at motels or hotels or share apartments. They suffer sexual harassment because some passengers consider them to be easy pick-ups rather than serious working women.

If a passenger makes unsolicited sexual remarks or asks that you meet him after the flight, I suggest employing assertive techniques, as described above in the section on sexual harassment. If he suggests socializing after the flight, you can tell him that your policy is not to date passengers. If he insists on grabbing, break away if necessary and ask him not to touch you. If he becomes unruly, call the captain or a member of the cockpit crew to speak to the passenger. It is illegal to disrupt the operations of the aircraft. An unruly passenger can be restrained in flight and arrested at the airport when the plane lands.

When you leave the airport, you should try not to be easily identified as a flight attendant. It may be best to change into street clothes before you depart. Another option is to leave the airport in groups. Your body language should indicate self-confidence, awareness, and alertness. Know the city and how to get around in it. The section in this chapter on traveling for business gives specific information.

If you share an out-of-town apartment with other airline personnel, special precautions should be taken to prevent theft and assault. Based on a group decision, security rules should be made up and adhered to by all; group security precautions work only if everyone practices them. Keys should be well guarded, not left where they can be found by a potential intruder. Agree not to have overnight guests unless everyone approves. Your bedroom should have its own lock to secure your personal possessions when you are away. I suggest securing your door with an auxiliary deadbolt lock and protecting the hinges if the hinge pins of the door are positioned on the frame outside your room. Keep your schedule and emergency numbers in a mutually acceptable safe place, out of the sight of visitors. By following these practices, you and your roommates can look after one another.

Social/Mental Health Workers

Social and mental health workers often meet with clients who are under a great deal of stress. The client is frequently frustrated and many times has been treated more like a number than like a person by the institutional bureaucracy.

Various safety precautions can reduce the risk of being assaulted by a client.

- Arrange your office furniture so that the client is not between you and the door. Never see a client with the door shut. Leave the door open, and make sure that you are within sight of a co-worker, or if this is not possible, at least be within call of a co-worker.

- Your body language should demonstrate confidence and self-assurance. Act toward your clients in a completely professional manner, treating them with respect and not permitting personal feelings or ego to get in the way.

- If the client is upset or seems angry, acknowledge this feeling and try to calm the situation. ("You seem upset. Is there anything I can do to help?"). If you are unable to lower the intensity of the situation and the client becomes hostile, leave immediately and get help.[10] If you are grabbed, break away. If you are assaulted and your life is threatened, fight back, incapacitating the attacker.

Chapter 6
The Rape Victim

Perhaps the best argument in favor of women learning self-defense is that rape is, in essence, a crime in which most assailants are never brought to justice. In a study of 1,401 cases of reported rape, in which the victims were taken to the emergency room of the Philadelphia General Hospital, only ninety-two men were convicted of rape—an appalling 6.6 percent.[1] And these were *reported* cases. Most rapes go unreported.

Why do so many rapists go free? Historically, when a man and woman entered into a marriage contract the women's body and access to it came under his exclusive jurisdiction. Rape was not a crime against the woman, but a crime against the male estate. In the same light, a virgin was considered the marketable property of her father. If she was deflowered, the merchandise was damaged and she was worth less. The laws were written to protect the value of the property, and in some cases the penalty for rape was death—not out of justice to the woman, but as a penalty for theft or damage of property.

Rape and the Law

It must be realized that rape laws still reflect this archaic thinking. In the eyes of the law and public in general, rape is still envisioned as a sexual crime. Traditionally, the law focuses on the behavior and and reputation of the victim—trying to ascertain whether or not she consented to the sexual act—as opposed to the behavior of the assailant. As I stated in Chapter 1, rape is and should be thought of as an assault, for which the motive is power and subjugation and in which the weapon used is sex. When rape is thought of as a sex crime, as it is in the eyes of the law, the issues become muddled. Reality is mixed with myth, and Victorian concepts of morality are often imposed on the victim.

We will first consider the laws surrounding rape, then proceed to some of the legal reforms taking place.

Traditional Rape Laws

The common-law definition of rape serves as the basis for most rape laws. Here rape is defined as unlawful carnal knowledge (sexual intercourse) by a man of a woman, not his wife, without the victim's consent. Specifically, there must be some penetration of the vagina by the penis, however slight. Other forms of sexual assault, such as oral and anal contact and the use of objects, are not included in this legal definition.

Consent.   In most states, the victim must prove that she did not consent to the act. The concept of consent is a feature unique to rape prosecution.[2] In the case of armed robbery, for example, the victim need not prove that she or he never consented to the crime. Yet, if a rape victim does not show evidence of physical violence, even if the assailant threatened her life with a weapon, her nonconsent may be questioned. In many states, "Her past sexual history can be introduced to show consent, as well as to undermine credibility."[3]

Corroboration.   Corroboration is testimony or evidence other than the testimony of the victim. Although not required in most states, it is often needed to get a rape conviction. Corroborative evidence may include torn clothing, bruises or injuries, medical evidence, promptness of complaint to friends, relatives, and/or the police, the emotional condition of the victim, and lack of reason to falsify charges.[4]

The Hale Instruction. In some states, judges are required to administer the Hale instruction to the jury. This caution to the jury, which dates back to the seventeeth century, is illustrative of the type of thinking that pervades the rape laws. The judge instructs the jury that "a charge such as that made against the defendant in this case is one which is easily made and, once made, difficult to defend against, even if the person accused is innocent. Therefore, the law requires that you examine the testimony of the female person named in the information with caution."[5] Although the Hale instruction is often quite damaging to the woman, this male fear of false accusation appears ungrounded. In statistics compiled from the New York City Police Department Sex Squad, it was found that the number of unfounded rape complaints (3.4 percent) was comparable to the number of unproven complaints of other felonies.[6]

Spousal Rape. Under common law, sexual intercourse between man and wife, although against the will of the wife, can never constitute rape. Intercourse is considered an inherent right of marriage where the wife is obligated to submit to the demands of her husband.

Bias Against the Victim. The following examples, although extreme, exemplify this bias in interpreting the law. In 1977, a sixteen-year-old girl who was wearing sneakers, blue jeans, and a blouse over a turtleneck sweater was raped in a high school stairwell in Wisconsin. The judge, Archie Simonson, sentenced the fifteen-year-old rapist to a year of court supervision in his own home. The judge's explanation of this lenient sentence was that due to the permissive climate of the community and the woman's revealing clothing, the boy was only behaving normally. (Simonson subsequently lost a recall election stemming from this incident.)[7] In 1978, a Hartford, Connecticut, judge dismissed a rape conspiracy charge, stating that "you can't blame somebody for trying." The assailant apparently was unable to commit the rape.[8] And, in Sweetwater County, Wyoming, the county attorney required rape victims to take lie-detector tests before he would prosecute their cases.[9]

Evidentiary Rules. Rules of evidence, which vary from state to state, have in some cases placed the *victim* on trial rather than the accused rapist. Although a man's sexual history, including prior charges and convictions for rape, may not be introduced in evidence if he doesn't take the witness stand,[10] testimony is often allowed regarding previous acts of intercourse between the offender and victim and between the victim and other men at different times in her life and regarding the general moral character of the victim.[11] As one victim put it, "I don't understand it. It was like I was the defendant and he was the plaintiff. I wasn't on trial. I don't see where I did anything wrong."[12]

Rape Law Reform

Largely through the efforts of the women's movement, rape became the focus of much attention in the 1970s, and the laws concerning rape have begun to be reformed. States that have led in the reform effort include California, Colorado, Florida, Michigan, and Wisconsin.

In 1974, Michigan adopted a rape law that has served as a model for a number of other states. The Michigan law expands the definition of sexual intercourse to include oral and anal sex and the use of objects. The burden of proving nonconsent is removed and corroboration is not required. The law is sexually neutral and the victim cannot be cross-examined about his or her reputation except under restricted circumstances.[13]

In California a number of laws concerning rape have been enacted in the past several years. Some of them deal with the rights of the victim. The use of the Hale instruction is prohibited, for example, and the use of the victim's past sexual history with persons other than the defendant is not allowed. Other laws deal with prosecution of rapists. One of these prohibits the granting of probation to a man convicted of rape by force or violence. And the definition of rape has been expanded to include the use of an object in an anal or vaginal opening.

In 1979, California joined several other states in enacting a spousal rape bill. In 1979, in Salem, Massachusetts, James Chretien was convicted of raping his wife and became the first man in U.S. history to be convicted of spousal rape.[14]

Although there has been legal reform, the law still focuses on victim consent, rather than on the behavior of the assailant. Only a few states have changed the definition of rape from a sexual crime to a crime of violence, and the biggest problem is getting the American public to identify rape in this way.

A woman in my class related the following incident:

The Postrape Victim

The friend of a brother of my roommate was visiting San Francisco. We went out to the beach at night. We were having a pleasant conversation so I felt no need to be on guard. He tried to kiss me and I simply refused. As we walked farther he suddenly started to pull at my clothes. I began to run. He caught me and continued. I screamed as loud as I could but the ocean drowned out my cries for help. There was no one in sight. I fought with my hands and nails, scratching his face. He pinned me down, kneeling on my thighs and holding my wrists. Each time I would scream he would throw sand in my mouth. He then raped me and I struggled and cried. Then he rolled over beside me. I was terrified to move but I had to get away. I quickly got up and searched for my clothes, keeping my eye on him. Apparently he had passed out. I wanted to crush his face with my foot. I wanted to run into the ocean and drown. I never felt like killing someone before. Nor had I ever felt suicidal before. This one act caused me to feel both. Yet something restrained my actions and I ran from my attacker toward the street and eventually found help.

I phoned the brother of my roommate. He came and got me. When I told him what had happened, he made a pass at me. I was insulted—insult upon injury. I came home, took a bath, and went to bed. The brother left that morning, found his friend, and I never saw the two of them again. The next day I told one of my roommates. I was extremely upset. She was understanding and suggested that I see a gynecologist. I did and was treated for crabs and some minor form of V.D. The physician reprimanded me for not going to the police. However, he was caring also in his treatment of me. It took a while, but I eventually bounced back emotionally and continued with my daily living. However, I've never forgotten it and can recall it as vividly as the day it happened. It will probably stay with me as long as I live.

Reactions to Rape

Rape victims suffer from severe trauma. The effects of rape may last for years, if not their entire lives. A common initial reaction is shock, which may manifest itself as crying, sobbing, or tenseness, or the feelings may be masked behind a calm composure.[15] During the first several weeks after the attack, the victim will experience a variety of reactions, depending upon the severity of the attack, where it took place, the type of emotional support and/or treatment the woman receives, and her own psychological state, among other things. A reaction that most rape victims experience is that of guilt.[16] Guilt arises for a variety of reasons, which all stem from society's perceptions of rape (see section on myths in Chapter 1). No matter what the victim has done or not done, she is blamed by society for the assault. She may feel guilty that she did not fight to the death (although her life probably was threatened), or that she did not know better, or that she was out late at night. She may also feel embarrassed and humiliated. As a result of the attack, the woman may suffer physical trauma (bruises, cuts, and soreness). She may also experience tension headaches and fatigue, nightmares and sleep disturbances, gastrointestinal irritability and genitourinary disturbance.[17] Phobic reactions are also possible: fear of being indoors or outdoors depending upon where she was attacked, fear of being alone, fear of people behind her, and the like.

After the initial postrape phase, the woman undergoes a long-term reorganization process. At this point she resumes what appears to be an outwardly normal life. She returns to work and tells others that she has coped with the rape and is all right now. She does not seek professional counseling. What really has happened is that she has blocked the psychological effects of the rape, preferring not to deal with it.[18] The victim may make changes in her life in order to feel safer, changing her telephone number to an unlisted one or changing her residence. The postrape victim may also experience nightmares and continue to experience phobias. Difficulty in her sex life may endure for a long period following the attack. Many relationships and marriages undergo a great strain as a result of the assault. The male partner may consider the woman to be "unclean" or blame her for the rape. The woman may have a long-term mistrust of any man.

Then there comes a point when many rape victims begin to deal with the pscyhological effects of the experience.[19] It happens when and if the woman begins to relive the rape and becomes aware of and angry about what was done to her. This is a very painful experience and is extremely depressing. It is during this period that the woman resolves negative feelings she has about herself, the fears that she has, and her anger toward the rapist. She struggles to become her own person again and gain control of her own life.[20] Women's support groups, rape counseling, and classes in self-defense against rape can be of great assistance toward this end.

Information for Rape Victims

Rape victims, as victims of violent crime, have the right to be treated with dignity. The following information will aid victims in reducing further trauma.

During the Rape. If you have chosen not to resist and if rape is imminent, try to concentrate on memorizing a description of the rapist. A good description will aid in his apprehension. Record his description as soon as possible (see Figure 6.1).

```
RACE_____ SEX_____ AGE_____ HEIGHT_____

WEIGHT_____ HAIR_____ EYES_____ COLOR_____

PHYSICAL CHARACTERISTICS (Describe build, scars, fingernails,
marks, tattoos, mustache, glasses, rings, etc.)

_____

CLOTHING (type and color; use diagram at left as a guide)

_____

WEAPONS (revolver, automatic, rifle, shotgun, knife, etc.)

_____

REMARKS (note anything suspect says, his accent, any
names used)

_____

MEANS OF EXCAPE, VEHICLE (license number, make, model,
year, color) or  ON FOOT (what direction)

_____
```

FIGURE 6.1. Description sheet for recording details about a rapist. The sheet should be filled out as soon as possible after the incident.

Immediately Following the Rape. Get to a safe place right away. Then call a friend and/or your local rape crisis line for support and information. *It is extremely important that you do this.* (A list of rape crisis lines across the country is given at the end of this chapter.) The rape crisis advocate will give you the information to help you decide your next steps.

You do not have to report the rape to the police—the decision is yours. Even if the authorities are supportive, proceeding through the legal system will be difficult and distressing. But if you choose to do so, you will be helping other women by at least making the police aware of the existence of this particular rapist and perhaps by having him arrested and sent to prison. It is difficult to give advice on this issue. Although I firmly believe in the concept of sending rapists to prison, I am aware of and empathetic to the plight of the victim. I don't feel that it is fair to put the victim through the additional severe trauma that often occurs in meeting with the police, the hospitals, and the courts. But each case differs; victims in some states receive better treatment and have a better chance of seeing the rapist convicted than in others. The choice is up to the individual.

If you decide to report the rape to the police, it is best to do so without delay (but after you have called the rape crisis line and/or a sympathetic friend to be with you). The crisis center can call the police for you if you desire. Do not shower, douche, or wash clothes, which will destroy evidence. You have a right to an explanation of police procedures and an explanation of any questions asked by the police. Some police officers are sympathetic to the plight of the victim, others are extremely insensitive. You do not have to answer questions that are irrelevant to the investigation of the crime. Make sure to read over the final police report before agreeing to sign it.

If you have reported the rape to the police, they will take you to the hospital either before or after questioning. You are not required to have the police present during the medical physical exam. The purpose of the medical exam is twofold: to treat the patient and to collect evidence. Evidence collected may include semen, fingernail scrapings, photographs of injuries, and clothing. Take a change of clothing because the police may want to keep yours for evidence.

Even if you don't report to the police, you will need some medical attention: tests for venereal disease and pregnancy, and examination and treatment for internal and external injuries. Have a friend or rape crisis advocate with you. Make sure you understand the purpose, side effects, and results of any procedures or medications given. The doctor may offer you DES, the "morning-after" pill. DES is a very potent synthetic hormone that is effective in preventing pregnancy, if taken within seventy-two hours of conception. It has, however, some violent side effects. Severe nausea and vomiting frequently occur, as well as water and salt retention, breast tenderness, abdominal and leg cramps, dizziness, headache, depression, rash, allergic reactions, and changes in blood-clotting time. There is also danger of birth defects and cancer.[21] Rather than taking DES, you may prefer to consider an alternative, such as waiting for your next menstrual period. Doctors can test for pregnancy within a month of conception. Early abortions can be performed in the doctor's office, relatively simply and inexpensively. Funding is commonly available through social service agencies and perhaps through government sources for victims of rape.

Some hospitals offer counseling services to rape victims. Check with the rape crisis advocate about counseling services and rap groups. She can also advise you of local self-defense courses for women.

The Courts

If you report the rape, it is the police and the district attorney who will decide whether or not the case will go to court. Because of the nature of rape laws, which require the prosecutor to prove that the victim did not consent to the act, in many states it is the victim who feels she is on trial, rather than the rapist. In many areas, the victim's name and address is read aloud in court, becoming public information. You may request that your name not be read.

If the district attorney decides to prosecute, at a preliminary hearing a judge will decide whether there will be a trial. The defense attorney will usually try to discredit the victim with the type of questioning designed to show consent to the rape or provocation of the attack. Depending upon the state laws, discussion of her sexual history may or may not be allowed. The defense lawyer may ask her if she wore a bra, or if she enjoyed being raped. Another obstacle the rape victim must encounter, if her case reaches this stage, is the jury. Juries reflect the same prejudices and biases as the rest of the community. They may blame the victim for the rape and be reluctant to send the assailant to prison, especially if the sentence is extremely harsh.

Judges, on the other hand, operate less on myth and prejudice than juries. Calven and Zeisel, of the University of Chicago Law School, examined 106 cases of rape. They compared the jury's decision to convict or acquit with a written statement from the judge on the case telling how he would have voted. In forty-two cases of simple rape (that is, not involving a weapon or a great deal of violence), the judge was 700 percent more likely to call it rape than the jury.[22]

Civil Suits

You personally can sue the rapist. This can be done even if the district attorney does not prosecute your case. You have the option of taking the rapist to civil court where you can sue him for damages. You may also be able to sue the owner of the property where the rape occurred if you can prove that some negligence on the owner's part contributed to the crime.

Rape Crisis Lines

This is a partial listing of rape crisis lines in the United States. If the rape hot line for your locality is not listed, call the information operator.

Alabama

Birmingham	(205) 323-RAPE	Los Angeles	(213) 262-0944
Mobile	(205) 473-RAPE	Marin County	(415) 294-2100
Alaska		Monterey	(408) 374-4357
Anchorage	(907) 276-RAPE	Palo Alto	(415) 493-RAPE
Arizona		Riverside	(714) 686-RAPE
Flagstaff	(602) 774-3351	Sacramento	(916) 447-RAPE
Phoenix	(602) 257-8095	San Diego	(714) 225-1243
Tucson	(602) 632-RAPE	San Francisco	(415) 647-RAPE
Arkansas		San Jose	(408) 287-3000
Little Rock	(501) 375-5181	San Mateo	(415) 349-RAPE
California		Santa Barbara	(805) 963-1696
Berkeley	(415) 845-RAPE	Santa Cruz	(408) 426-RAPE
El Cajon	(714) 466-RAPE	Sonoma County	(707) 545-RAPE
Fresno	(209) 222-RAPE	Stockton	(209) 465-RAPE

Colorado			*Michigan*	
Denver	(303) 321-8191		Lansing	(517) 337-1717
Pueblo	(303) 545-9990		Ypsilanti	(313) 994-1616
Connecticut			*Minnesota*	
New Haven	(203) 397-2273		Minneapolis	(612) 825-4357
Hartford	(203) 522-6666		St. Paul	(612) 298-5898
Delaware			*Mississippi*	
Wilmington	(302) 658-5011		Jackson	(601) 354-1113
District of Columbia	(202) 387-7798		*Missouri*	
Florida			Kansas City	(816) 923-1123
Gainesville	(904) 377-RAPE		Saint Louis	(314) 725-2010
Jacksonville	(904) 384-2232		*Montana*	
Miami	(305) 325-6949		Billings	(406) 259-6506
Georgia			Missoula	(406) 543-8277
Atlanta	(404) 659-RAPE		*Nebraska*	
Hawaii			Lincoln	(402) 475-RAPE
Honolulu	(808) 244-3748		Omaha	(402) 345-RAPE
Maui	(808) 244-3748		*Nevada*	
Idaho			Las Vegas	(702) 735-1111
Boise	(208)345-RAPE		Reno	(702) 329-RAPE
Illinois			*New Hampshire*	
Champaign	(217) 384-4444		Manchester	(603) 668-2299
Chicago	(312) 372-6600		*New Jersey*	
Iowa			New Brunswick	(201) 828-RAPE
Ames	(515) 292-1101		Trenton	(609) 989-RAPE
Des Moines	(515) 262-4357		*New Mexico*	
Iowa City	(319) 338-4800		Albuquerque	(505) 247-0707
Kansas			Santa Fe	(505) 982-4667
Lawrence	(913) 843-8985		*New York*	
Topeka	(913) 295-8499		Buffalo	(716) 838-5980
Wichita	(316) 263-3002		New York City	(212) 777-4000
Kentucky			Rochester	(716) 546-2595
Louisville	(502) 581-RAPE		*North Carolina*	
Louisiana			Chapel Hill	(919) 967-RAPE
Baton Rouge	(504) 383-RAPE		Raleigh	(919) 782-3060/829-1373
New Orleans	(504) 821-6000		*North Dakota*	
Maine			Fargo	(701) 293-RAPE
Portland	(207) 773-5516		Grand Forks	(701) 746-6666
Maryland			*Ohio*	
Baltimore	(301) 366-RAPE		Akron	(216) 434-RAPE
Cheverly	(301) 341-4942		Cincinnati	(513) 381-5610
Massachusetts			Cleveland	(216) 391-3912
Cambridge	(617) 492-RAPE		Columbus	(614) 221-4447
Pittsfield	(413) 443-0089		Springfield	(513) 325-3707

Oklahoma	
Oklahoma City	(405) 524-RAPE
Oregon	
Portland	(503) 235-5333
Salem	(503) 399-7722
Pennsylvania	
Philadelphia	(215) 922-3434
Pittsburgh	(412) 765-2731
Rhode Island	
Providence	(401) 861-4040
South Carolina	
Charleston	(803) 722-RAPE
Greenville	(803) 232-8633
South Dakota	
Sioux Falls	(605) 334-7022
Tennessee	
Knoxville	(615) 522-RAPE
Memphis	(901) 527-4747
Nashville	(615) 327-1110
Texas	
Austin	(512) 472-RAPE
Dallas	(214) 521-1020

Fort Worth	(817) 334-0251
Houston	(214) 521-1020
Utah	
Salt Lake City	(801) 532-RAPE
Vermont	
Burlington	(802) 863-1236
Virginia	
Alexandria	(703) 548-3810
Norfolk	(804) 622-4300
Richmond	(804) 648-9224
Roanoke	(703) 981-9351
Washington	
Renton	(206) 226-RAPE
Seattle	(206) 632-RAPE
Spokane	(509) 624-RAPE
Wisconsin	
Madison	(608) 251-RAPE
Milwaukee	(414) 278-4617
Wyoming	
Cheyenne	(307) 632-2666
Rock Springs	(307) 382-4381

Notes

1. National Commission on the Observance of International Women's Year, *Rape* (Washington, D.C.: U.S. Government Printing Office, 1977), p. 3.

2. Subcommittee on Domestic and International Scientific Planning, Analysis and Cooperation, *Research into Violent Behavior: Overview and Sexual Assaults*, statement of Dr. Martha Burt (Washington, D.C.: U.S. Government Printing Office, 1978), p. 305.

3. *Crime on the Streets 1978*, F.B.I. Uniform Crime Report (Washington, D.C.: U.S. Government Printing Office, 1979).

4. Burt, in *Research into Violent Behavior*, p. 312.

5. Ibid., p. 307.

6. Ibid., statement of William Fuller, p. 675.

7. Ibid., statement of Dr. Nicholas Groth, pp. 452–55.

8. Ibid., statement of Dr. Martha Burt, p. 308.

9. Ibid., p. 312.

10. Ibid., p. 305.

11. Ibid., p. 312.

12. Ibid.

13. San Francisco Women Against Rape, *Not a Fleeting Rage: A Handbook on Rape* (San Francisco, 1977), p. 27.

14. Burt, in *Research into Violent Behavior*, p. 312.

15. Ibid., pp. 314–15.

16. Maureen Green, "Children's Stories Offer Stereotypes," *Womenews*, vol. 5, no. 1, March 1980.

17. F. Javorek and L. A. Lyon, "California Personality Inventory Factor Structure for Targets of Rape vs. a General Population of Women," unpublished, Research Bulletin 75-3, 1975, Violence Research Unit, Denver General Hospital.

18. A. Medea and K. Thompson, *Against Rape* (New York: Noonday Press, 1974), p. 11.

19. Burt, in *Research into Violent Behavior*, p. 307.

Chapter 2

1. James Selkin, "Behavioral Analysis of Rape," unpublished research report, Violence Research Unit, Denver General Hospital, p. 3.

2. James Selkin, "Don't Take It Lying Down," *Psychology Today*, January 1975, p. 72.

3. Julius Fast, *Body Language* (New York: Simon and Schuster, 1970).

4. Subcommittee on Domestic and International Scientific Planning, Analysis and Cooperation, *Research into Violent Behavior: Overview and Sexual Assaults* (Washington, D.C.: U.S. Government Printing Office, 1978) statement of Dr. Martha Burt, p. 312.

5. Andra Medea, and K. Thompson, *Against Rape* (New York: Farrar, Straus and Giroux, 1974), p. 36.

6. National Institute of Mental Health, *Victims of Rape* (Washington, D.C.: U.S. Government Printing Office, 1978), p. 28.

7. Burt, in *Research into Violent Behavior*, p. 308.

8. Queen's Bench Foundation, *Rape: Prevention and Resistance* (San Francisco, 1976).

9. Pauline Bart, "Avoiding Rape: A Comparative Study," unpublished paper presented at the International Sociological Association, Uppsala, Sweden, August 1978, p. 9.

10. Selkin, "Behavioral Analysis," p. 9.

11. James Selkin, "Protecting Personal Space: Victim and Resister Reactions to Assaultive Rape," *Journal of Community Psychology*, 6, (1978): p. 267.

12. Menachim Amir, *Patterns in Forcible Rape* (Chicago: University of Chicago Press, 1971).

13. Selkin, "Behavioral Analysis," p. 7.

14. Bart, "Avoiding Rape," p. 9.

15. Ibid., p. 21.

16. Selkin, "Behavioral Analysis," p. 9.

17. Susan Brownmiller, *Against Our Will* (New York: Simon and Schuster, 1975), p. 402.

18. Phyllis Chesler, *Women and Madness* (New York: Avon Books, 1972), pp. 289–90.

19. Brownmiller, *Against Our Will*. p. 402.

20. F. Javorek and L. A. Lyon, "California Personality Inventory Factor

Structure for Targets of Rape vs. a General Population of Women," unpublished Research Bulletin 75-3, Violence Research Unit, Denver General Hospital, 1975, p. 8.

21. Selkin, "Behavioral Analysis," p. 3.

22. Ibid., p. 358.

1. Liddon R. Griffith, *Mugging: You Can Protect Yourself* (Englewood Cliffs, N.J.: Prentice-Hall, 1978), p. 6.

2. Mary Conroy and E. Ritvo, *Common Sense Self-Defense* (St. Louis: The C. V. Mosby Co., 1977), p. 34.

3. Eugene A. Sloane, *The Complete Book of Locks, Keys, Burglar and Smoke Alarms and Other Security Devices* (New York: William Morrow and Co., 1977), p. 96.

1. Betty L. Harragan, *Games Mother Never Taught You* (New York: Warner Books, 1977), p. 366.

2. Barbara A. Gutek and C. Nakamura, "Sexuality and the Workplace," paper presented at the annual convention of the American Psychological Association, New York, September 1979.

3. *San Francisco Examiner,* 20 April 1980.

4. Harragan, *Games.*

5. Ibid., p. 367.

6. *San Francisco Examiner,* 15 October 1979.

7. Ibid., 11 March 1980.

8. James Selkin, "Don't Take It Lying Down," *Psychology Today,* January 1975, pp. 71–76.

9. Janet Whitman, "Patient Attacks. Self-Protection When Violence Looms," *RN Magazine,* September 1979, pp. 31–33.

10. Ibid.

1. William Krasner, L. Meyer, and N. Carroll, *Victims of Rape,* National Institute of Mental Health (Washington, D.C.: U.S. Government Printing Office, 1977), p. 29.

2. National Commission on the Observance of International Women's Year, *Rape* (Washington, D.C.: U.S. Government Printing Office, 1977), p. 7.

3. Ibid., p. 7.

4. Ibid., p. 8.

5. California Commission on the Status of Women, Legislative Summary, October 1975, p. 14.

6. National Commission on the Observance of International Women's Year, *Rape,* p. 9.

Chapter 4

Chapter 5

Chapter 6

7. *San Francisco Examiner*, 13 August 1978.

8. *San Jose Mercury*, 2 June 1978.

9. *San Francisco Examiner*, 28 August 1979.

10. Susan Brownmiller, *Against Our Will* (New York: Simon and Schuster, 1975), p. 372.

11. Ibid., p. 371.

12. Ibid., p. 373.

13. National Commission on the Observance of International Women's Year, *Rape*, p. 12.

14. *San Francisco Chronicle*, 30 September 1979.

15. Ann Burgess and L. Holmstrom, "Rape Trauma Syndrome," *American Journal of Psychiatry* 131, no. 9 (September 1974): 982.

16. Ibid., p. 983; Queen's Bench Foundation, *Rape Victimization Study* (San Francisco, 1975), p. 16; Andra Medea and K. Thompson, *Against Rape* (New York: Noonday Press, 1974), pp. 104–105.

17. Burgess, "Rape Trauma Syndrome."

18. Medea, *Against Rape*, p. 102.

19. Ibid., p. 103.

20. Ibid., p. 106.

21. San Francisco Women Against Rape. pp. 15–16.

22. Subcommittee on Domestic and International Scientific Planning, Analysis and Cooperation of the Committee on Science and Technology, U.S. House of Representatives, 95th Congress, Second Session, *Research into Violent Behavior: Overview and Sexual Assaults* (Washington, D.C.: U.S. Government Printing Office, 1978), statement of Dr. Martha Burt, p. 319.

Index